Crimes Against Women

CRIME, JUSTICE, AND PUNISHMENT

Crimes Against Women

Gerda Gallop-Goodman

Austin Sarat, GENERAL EDITOR

CHELSEA HOUSE PUBLISHERS
Philadelphia

Chelsea House Publishers

Editor in Chief Sally Cheney
Director of Production Kim Shinners
Manufacturing Manager Diann Grasse
Creative Manager Takeshi Takahashi
Executive Editor Lee Marcott
Production Assistant Jaimie Winkler

Layout by 21st Century Publishing and
Communications, Inc., New York, N.Y.

First Printing

1 3 5 7 9 8 6 4 2

The Chelsea House World Wide Web address is
http://www.chelseahouse.com

Library of Congress Cataloging-in-Publication Data

Gallop-Goodman, Gerda
    Crimes against women / Gerda Gallop-Goodman.
        p. cm — (Crime, justice, and punishment)
    Includes bibliographical references and index.
    ISBN 0-7910-4255-3 (alk. paper)
        1. Women—Crimes against—United States—Juve-
    nile literature. 2. Wife abuse—United States—Juvenile
    literature. 3. Rape—United States—Juvenile literature.
    [1. Women—Crimes against. 2. Wife abuse. 3. Rape.
    4. Violent crimes.] I. Title. II. Series.

HV6250.4.W65 G35 2001
362.88'082'0973—dc21
                                    2001028480

Contents

CRIME, JUSTICE, AND PUNISHMENT

Fears and Fascinations:

An Introduction to
Crime, Justice, and Punishment

By Austin Sarat

We live with crime and images of crime all around us. Crime evokes in most of us a deep aversion, a feeling of profound vulnerability, but it also evokes an equally deep fascination. Today, in major American cities the fear of crime is a major fact of life, some would say a disproportionate response to the realities of crime. Yet the fear of crime is real, palpable in the quickened steps and furtive glances of people walking down darkened streets. At the same time, we eagerly follow crime stories on television and in movies. We watch with a "who done it" curiosity, eager to see the illicit deed done, the investigation undertaken, the miscreant brought to justice and given his just deserts. On the streets the presence of crime is a reminder of our own vulnerability and the precariousness of our taken-for-granted rights and freedoms. On television and in the movies the crime story gives us a chance to probe our own darker motives, to ask "Is there a criminal within?" as well as to feel the collective satisfaction of seeing justice done.

Fear and fascination, these two poles of our engagement with crime, are, of course, only part of the story. Crime is, after all, a major social and legal problem, not just an issue of our individual psychology. Politicians today use our fear of, and fascination with, crime for political advantage. How we respond to crime, as well as to the political uses of the crime issue, tells us a lot about who we are as a people as well as what we value and what we tolerate. Is our response compassionate or severe? Do we seek to understand or to punish, to enact an angry vengeance or to rehabilitate and welcome the criminal back into our midst? The CRIME, JUSTICE, AND PUNISHMENT series is designed to explore these themes, to ask why we are fearful and fascinated, to probe the meanings and motivations of crimes and criminals and of our responses to them, and, finally, to ask what we can learn about ourselves and the society in which we live by examining our responses to crime.

Crime is always a challenge to the prevailing normative order and a test of the values and commitments of law-abiding people. It is sometimes a Raskolnikov-like act of defiance, an assertion of the unwillingness of some to live according to the rules of conduct laid out by organized society. In this sense, crime marks the limits of the law and reminds us of law's all-too-regular failures. Yet sometimes there is more desperation than defiance in criminal acts; sometimes they signal a deep pathology or need in the criminal. To confront crime is thus also to come face-to-face with the reality of social difference, of class privilege and extreme deprivation, of race and racism, of children neglected, abandoned, or abused whose response is to enact on others what they have experienced themselves. And occasionally crime, or what is labeled a criminal act, represents a call for justice, an appeal to a higher moral order against the inadequacies of existing law.

Figuring out the meaning of crime and the motivations of criminals and whether crime arises from defiance, desperation, or the appeal for justice is never an easy task. The motivations and meanings of crime are as varied as are the persons who engage in criminal conduct. They are as mysterious as any of the mysteries of the human soul. Yet the desire to know the secrets of crime and the criminal is a strong one, for in that knowledge may lie one step on the road to protection, if not an assurance of one's own personal safety. Nonetheless, as strong as that desire may be, there is no available technology that can allow us to know the whys of crime with much confidence, let alone a scientific certainty. We can, however, capture something about crime by studying the defiance, desperation, and quest for justice that may be associated with it. Books in the CRIME, JUSTICE, AND PUNISHMENT series will take up that challenge. They tell stories of crime and criminals, some famous, most not, some glamorous and exciting, most mundane and commonplace.

This series will, in addition, take a sober look at American criminal justice, at the procedures through which we investigate crimes and identify criminals, at the institutions in which innocence or guilt is determined. In these procedures and institutions we confront the thrill of the chase as well as the challenge of protecting the rights of those who defy our laws. It is through the efficiency and dedication of law enforcement that we might capture the criminal; it is in the rare instances of their corruption or brutality that we feel perhaps our deepest betrayal. Police, prosecutors, defense lawyers, judges, and jurors administer criminal justice and in their daily actions give substance to the guarantees of the Bill of Rights. What is an adversarial system of justice? How does it work? Why do we have it? Books in the CRIME, JUSTICE, AND PUNISHMENT series will examine the thrill of the chase as we seek to capture the criminal. They will also reveal the drama and majesty of the criminal trial as well as the day-to-day reality of a criminal justice system in which trials are the exception and negotiated pleas of guilty are the rule.

When the trial is over or the plea has been entered, when we have separated the innocent from the guilty, the moment of punishment has arrived. The injunction to punish the guilty, to respond to pain inflicted by inflicting pain, is as old as civilization itself. "An eye for an eye and a tooth for a tooth" is a biblical reminder that punishment must measure pain for pain. But our response to the criminal must be better than and different from the crime itself. The biblical admonition, along with the constitutional prohibition of "cruel and unusual punishment," signals that we seek to punish justly and to be just not only in the determination of who can and should be punished, but in how we punish as well. But neither reminder tells us what to do with the wrongdoer. Do we rape the rapist, or burn the home of the arsonist? Surely justice and decency say no. But, if not, then how can and should we punish? In a world in which punishment is neither identical to the crime nor an automatic response to it, choices must be made and we must make them. Books in the CRIME, JUSTICE, AND PUNISHMENT series will examine those choices and the practices, and politics, of punishment. How do we punish and why do we punish as we do? What can we learn about the rationality and appropriateness of today's responses to crime by examining our past and its responses? What works? Is there, and can there be, a just measure of pain?

CRIME, JUSTICE, AND PUNISHMENT brings together books on some of the great themes of human social life. The books in this series capture our fear and fascination with crime and examine our responses to it. They remind us of the deadly seriousness of these subjects. They bring together themes in law, literature, and popular culture to challenge us to think again, to think anew, about subjects that go to the heart of who we are and how we can and will live together.

*   *   *   *   *

Becoming the victim of a crime is by no means a random event. Studies show that we are much more likely to be victimized by someone of our own race than by someone of a different race. In addition, we are more likely to be violently attacked by someone we know, indeed even someone we may love, than by a predatory stranger. For a long time societies denied this fact, choosing to leave crimes perpetrated by intimates in the domain of privacy. This left women with little or no legal recourse when they were criminally assaulted. Sadly, such assaults happen all too often.

Crimes Against Women is a compelling and comprehensive overview of the ways women become crime victims, particularly crimes involving domestic and sexual violence. It explores the special vulnerability of women due both to their traditional roles in the family and to the law's traditional indifference to domestic violence. Using tragic case histories and a deft historical sensibility, Gerda Gallop-Goodman gives her readers a close-up view of the reality behind the statistics. In addition, she addresses the steps that the legal system is taking to deal with crimes against women. The writing is animated by a clear vision and a commitment to making society safer for all its citizens.

Violence
Against
Women

It was publicized as the crime of the century. Nicole Brown Simpson was the young, beautiful mother of two children and the ex-wife of National Football League legend, actor, and sports commentator O. J. Simpson; on June 12, 1994, Nicole Simpson and her friend Ron Goldman were brutally murdered in front of her Brentwood, California, home. The two were stabbed repeatedly, Nicole Simpson's head was nearly severed from her shoulders. In October 1995 O. J. Simpson was acquitted of these murders, but he was found liable for their deaths in a 1997 civil trial.

What led to O. J. Simpson's arrest and subsequent murder charges? He had a history of battery of his ex-wife, Nicole. Over the course of the murder trial, Americans heard 911 calls Nicole Simpson made to police pleading for help as her ex-husband's cursing, yelling, and sounds of physical violence were audible in the background. She had reportedly called a battered women's shelter five days before her death in terror that

13

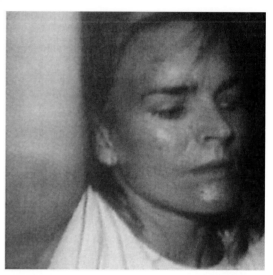

During the Simpsons' marriage, police had arrested O. J. at least eight times for domestic violence; neighbors had seen Nicole's black eyes. She had told friends and family members that she feared her ex-husband, and that she felt he was going to kill her. These photographs of Nicole were presented during the murder trial.

O. J. Simpson was going to kill her.

Even during the Simpsons' marriage, police had arrested O. J. at least eight times for domestic violence; neighbors had seen Nicole's black eyes. And once the couple divorced in 1992, he continued to assault, threaten, stalk, and intimidate her. She had told friends and family members that she feared her ex-husband, and that she felt he was going to kill her. She had written detailed descriptions of physical attacks by O. J. Simpson in a diary. Yet such evidence was ruled hearsay and disallowed from being presented at the murder trial.

Each year, 2 million women are beaten by their partners and more than 500,000 women report being raped or sexually assaulted. Some estimates indicate there might be as many as 4 million victims of domestic violence each year. The Federal Bureau of Investigation and the Justice Department estimate that a woman is beaten every 15 seconds in the United States. Because of the intimate nature of these crimes against women, many are unaware of just how widespread they are.

According to the U. S. Department of Justice's National Crime Victimization Survey, from 1998 to 1999 there were about 21.2 million property crimes (burglary, motor vehicle, household theft), 7.4 million violent crimes (rape or sexual assault, robbery, aggravated assault, simple assault), and 0.2 million personal thefts (pick pocketing, purse snatching). In 1998, there were an estimated 16,914 murders in the U.S. compared with 15,561 during 1999. Males account for about 75 percent of all murder victims. Males were victims of overall violent crime, robbery, aggravated assault, and simple assault at rates higher than females in 1999. Males experienced violent crime at rates 28 percent greater (37 compared to 29 victimizations per 1,000), and were robbed at rates more than twice that (five robberies per 1,000 compared to two) of females. Not surprisingly, females were victims of rape and sexual assault at 7.5 times greater the rate of males. In 1999, three females per 1,000 were raped or sexually assaulted compared with 0.4 males per 1,000.

Even when the level of exposure to crime is low, women and older people are considerably more fearful of crime than men and younger people. Women are also more likely to alter their behavior because they fear becoming victims of a crime. The contradiction between the victimization rates and levels of fear among women and the elderly is known as "the paradox of fear." In other words, fear of crime is out of proportion to the probability of becoming a victim. For example, most findings show that the crimes people fear the most—murder and other violent crime—are less likely to occur than property crimes.

Research on fear of crime has yet to pinpoint this phenomenon—the contradiction between victimization rates and fear of crime among women. Some arguments include the fact that women's fear of crime is related to the fear of rape and to women's socialization, which may increase the perceived seriousness of this crime even at lower levels of objective risk. Others argue that very few studies show an understanding of how class, race, and gender relations influence fear of crime or how such fear affects the lives of women of different racial, ethnic, and socioeconomic backgrounds. Many studies are based on official statistics, which do not classify incidents of domestic violence or sexual harassment as crimes.

Domestic violence is actual or threatened physical or sexual violence, economic abuse, psychological abuse, or emotional abuse with the effect of establishing power and control over another person through fear and intimidation. Other terms used to describe domestic violence include intimate partner violence, spousal abuse, and battering. Domestic partners include current or former spouses, boyfriends, or girlfriends.

Abusers include boyfriends, same-sex partners, and roommates, and can be of any age, race, and background. One third of women who are physically abused by a husband or boyfriend grew up in a household in which their mother was abused. About one in five were abused as children.

Physical abuse includes hitting, slapping, kicking, biting, pushing, shoving, punching, choking, and other ways of physically harming a person. It may involve being hit with a weapon, such as a knife or gun. Some

victims are tied up and held, some are left in dangerous places.

Susan Hansen, a housewife, suffered abuse for 11 years until she left her husband James and sought help in a Fort Lauderdale, Florida, shelter. Hansen had no job skills and four small children. She was emotionally and financially dependent on her husband, and believed that staying with her abusive husband was better for her children than living as a single parent on her own. The abuse was usually precipitated by her husband's drinking and happened only occasionally at first. Then it became a daily cycle of verbal abuse with claims that she was an inadequate mother, wife, or housekeeper. Hansen was stripped of her self-esteem and her dignity.

Domestic violence is actual or threatened physical, psychological, or emotional abuse with the effect of establishing power and control over another person through fear and intimidation. One third of women who are physically abused by a husband or boyfriend grew up in a household in which their mother was abused. About one in five were abused as children.

At one point, James threw a knife at her in an attempt to kill her; it just missed her head. Then her husband turned his violence toward their children—they were beaten and whipped almost daily. On the night her husband almost killed her with the knife, she decided to leave with her children and turn her life around. She didn't know where to go or to whom to turn, and sought refuge with a friend who helped her find a shelter for abused women. Today, Hansen and her children are safe.

Domestic violence is more than physical abuse. It also includes sexual abuse, defined as when a person is forced to participate in a sexual situation against their will. It can mean pursuing sexual activity when the victim is not fully conscious, is not asked for consent, has said no, or is afraid to say no.

Women often can't afford to leave their abusers, especially if they have children. They're economically dependent on their husbands, and that economic leverage is part of the control exerted by the batterer. Often the batterer controls all of the finances. If she attempts to leave, or talks about leaving or divorcing him, the batterer convinces her that she won't be able to afford legal help if she tries to get out of the relationship or that she will be left with nothing.

Michelle, a client of Women Against Abuse, a 25-year-old organization that operates a shelter for battered women in Philadelphia, was going through the legal process of filing a case against her abusive husband of 18 years. One day, Michelle was accompanied by Nichelle Mitchem, the organization's director, to the grocery store to purchase cereal for her children. Standing in front of the shelves of cereal, Michelle began crying hysterically. She felt overwhelmed by all of the choices of cereal. She literally had not been shopping in 18 years. Her husband constantly berated her, telling her she was stupid. She was not allowed to have money or to make any decisions for herself or her children—

even to purchase groceries for her family.

Another way an abuser dominates his wife or girl-friend is by psychological or emotional abuse, which involves threatening (sometimes with a weapon), intimidating, humiliating, yelling, blaming, or making the victim feel inferior, stupid, or emotionally hurt. Victims can also be deprived of things they need, or they can be kept away from other people. The serious emotional and psychological results of spousal abuse are often the most severe consequences of such violence. Victims are frequently abused in more than one manner at the same time. Battering does not occur from the abuser's momentary loss of temper. In fact, one in five women victimized by their spouses or ex-spouses report they have been victimized over and over again by the same person. Battering is the establishment of control and fear in a relationship through violence and other forms of abuse. To coerce and control, the batterer uses acts of violence and a series of behaviors, including intimidation, threats, psychological abuse, and isolation.

Battering can escalate into life-threatening danger. The incidence of battering is difficult to measure for many reasons. For example, studies indicate that doctors are still untrained and unable to recognize that a woman who shows up in the emergency room with signs of abuse may be making a plea for help. About 20 percent of all female victims of domestic violence seek medical assistance; 37 percent of women who sought treatment in emergency rooms for violence-related injuries in 1994 were injured by a current or former spouse, boyfriend, or girlfriend.

According to the National Crime Victimization Survey, published by the U.S. Department of Justice, nearly 1 million incidents of domestic violence occurred each year from 1992 to 1996, and 85 percent of victims were women. On average, each year from 1992 to 1996, approximately eight in 1,000 women

According to the National Crime Victimization Survey, published by the U.S. Department of Justice, nearly 1 million incidents of domestic violence occurred each year from 1992 to 1996, and 85 percent of victims were women. These marchers are participating in a 1997 "Silent Witness" march and vigil to honor the memory of 39 women who lost their lives in South Carolina due to domestic violence.

experienced a violent episode perpetrated by a current or former spouse, boyfriend, or girlfriend.

The incidence of domestic violence has been declining for women, yet the numbers are no less startling. In 1996, women reported 840,000 incidents by a partner, down from 1.1 million in 1993. In 1996, about 2,000 murders were attributed to intimate partners, down from 3,000 in 1976. Nearly three out of four involved a female victim. Certain groups of women who may be at higher risk for abuse include women who are single, separated, or divorced (or planning separation or divorce); are between the ages of 17 and

28; abuse alcohol or other drugs or have partners who do; are pregnant; or have partners who are excessively jealous or possessive.

Louis and Sylvia had a volatile relationship. Louis was extremely violent toward Sylvia and had a temper that flared without warning. Because he was emotionally dependent on Sylvia, he would fly into fits of jealous rage. The thought of her leaving terrified Louis. He blamed Sylvia for his dependency on her—and for his violence—and took it out on her with regular beatings. Louis tracked Sylvia's every move. He called her frequently from work to check up on her and to make sure that she was at the location where she said she would be. Although Louis was generous—he bought Sylvia expensive jewelry and clothing and took her to expensive restaurants—he was extremely jealous. He despised other men "eyeing his woman" and was obsessed with this. Her every movement had to be kept under his control.

In April 1999, Carlos Angel Diaz Santiago, 22, jumped into a borrowed car and chased the car of his former girlfriend, Candace Wertz, 20, through the streets of Sinking Spring, Pennsylvania. Along for the ride with Wertz were her two-year-old son, a girlfriend, Cynthia Jacques, 22, and Jacques's two-year-old daughter. While Wertz tried to make a desperate 911 call to police on her cell phone, Santiago pushed his car into Wertz's, bumping it onto railroad tracks into the path of a freight train. Wertz and her three companions were killed. Santiago was charged with criminal homicide. Ironically, Wertz had a protection order against Santiago that had just expired. Relatives and neighbors said they saw it coming. Wertz, who feared for her life, had been beaten by Santiago for years. Despite her efforts, Wertz couldn't get away from him.

Courts can provide protection to battered women by issuing restraining orders (including no-contact orders, orders of protection, and antiharassment orders), which require that the batterer stay away from the battered woman. States vary in the particular types of orders that they issue: it usually depends on the relationship between the batterer and the battered woman, the severity and history of violence, and the type of protection the battered woman wants. Violating such restraining orders is a criminal offense, and can lead to incarceration. It has been found in one study that although not all batterers honor restraining orders, such orders do reduce violence, at least in the short run. In the study, 34 percent of batterers didn't honor the restraining order. If the batterer was unemployed, the violation rate was 83 percent; if the batterer had a prior criminal record, all who had been served a restraining order violated it. But protection orders do deter a large percentage of batterers.

Wertz wasn't a celebrity, but she shared something in common with the experience of some public figures—stalking. Because celebrities are always in the limelight and fans are given a certain level of access to them through Web sites, magazines, TV, talk shows, and fan clubs, they are frequent targets of stalkers.

One infamous incident of celebrity stalking occurred in 1989. Teenager Robert Bardo became infatuated with Rebecca Schaeffer, an actress on a popular TV sitcom My Sister Sam. To Bardo, Schaeffer personified a goddess, and he worshipped her. Bardo sent the actress fan mail after watching her on the TV show. She responded by sending Bardo a handwritten postcard thanking him for his letters. Soon Bardo, living in a world of fantasy and mentally ill, traveled from his home in Arizona to visit Schaeffer in California in June 1987. After two unsuccessful attempts (once armed with a knife) to see Schaeffer at the studio where My Sister Sam was filmed, Bardo returned to Arizona.

Two years later, and no less infatuated, Bardo paid a private detective $250 for Schaeffer's home address. He got the idea from reading about how a stalker was able to get the address of an actress. Bardo's infatuation for Schaeffer, however, had turned to contempt after he saw her appearance in a sexually explicit film. He was convinced Schaeffer had become just "another Hollywood whore."

Bardo set out to see Schaeffer again, this time armed with a gun purchased by his older brother, since Bardo was not yet 21. He wandered throughout Schaeffer's neighborhood before arriving at her front door. When she appeared at the door, he handed her another one of his handwritten letters. Schaeffer assumed he was a messenger. About an hour later, Bardo returned to her door. This time, he shot her in the chest when she opened the door. Schaeffer died and Bardo got away, but he was later captured and sentenced to life in prison without parole.

Stalking doesn't just occur among celebrities, however. Formerly married couples or people who have dated each other, like Wertz, can become stalked. Upset over the end of a relationship, obsessive stalkers have often resorted to following the victim, frequently driving by their residence, breaking into their car or home, hiding in the victim's car, vandalizing the victim's car or home, phoning or writing obscene messages, or taunting the victim with threats of violence (including murder). Stalking, or repeated harassing or threatening behavior, is a form of domestic violence. In a national study, an estimated 1 million women were stalked annually. Women made up the majority (78 percent) of all stalking victims, and most perpetrators were men (87 percent). Women (60 percent) are more likely to be stalked by intimate partners. Approximately 80 percent of women who are stalked by former husbands are physically assaulted by that partner, and 30 percent are sexually assaulted by that partner.

Sexual assault is a devastating crime against women.

Rape is the forced participation of a victim in a sexual situation against their will. According to The National Crime Victimization Survey, 172,400 women were victims of rape from 1992 to 1993. There were 71 forcible rapes per 100,000 females reported to U.S. law enforcement agencies in 1996. Women die as a result of rape in about 0.1 percent of all cases.

Stranger rape is the type of rape most people think of when referring to rape. A menacing, unknown man hides behind the bushes in the dark waiting for a female he has been stalking for weeks—following her to and from work, watching her through the windows of her home, calculating her every move. As she returns home late at night from work, she is taken by surprise as he pounces on her with knife in hand, forces her inside her home, and proceeds to rape her despite her screams in protest. The perpetrator threatens to kill her if she doesn't stop resisting or screaming, so the victim must lie in silence or possibly lose her life. The perpetrator flees into the night as the victim lies crumpled on the floor—terrified and violated. Contrary to popular belief, stranger rape is usually preplanned, not a random act of violence. The victim is usually someone whom the rapist has targeted.

In about 25 percent of cases, rape is spontaneous—the perpetrator may have been drinking or in the midst of committing another crime. The victim is usually caught off guard and may or may not resist the attack, depending on how terrified she is and whether she perceives that it may help. The rapist is an unknown man who often uses a weapon to threaten and coerce the victim. It can occur anywhere. The victim can be forced to perform or submit to any physical act of a sexual nature, including sexual intercourse.

Date or acquaintance rape, a subcategory of rape, involves sexual assault, physical violence, and verbal or emotional abuse. The perpetrator is not a stranger to the victim; the victim and perpetrator may have attended the same party or social event, dated, met at a bar and left together, or lived together as an unmarried couple. The perpetrator may also be a coworker or neighbor—someone the victim is familiar with, but with whom she doesn't necessarily have a social relationship. Because of the familiarity with the perpetrator, the victim feels a sense of security or trust. Like stranger rape, the perpetrator has planned to commit the rape with a targeted victim by luring her into a location or scenario where no one will suspect anything wrong will take place. He is intent on achieving sexual domination over this victim—by violent means—perhaps because he has been "wronged" in some way and the victim is the one who will pay. Perhaps he feels she has "led him on," or turned him down for a date. A perpetrator of date rape rarely uses a weapon or threats of violence. Often date rape involves alcohol and/or drugs.

Date rape is prevalent on college campuses where it occurs among students who are friends, couples, acquaintances, or who attend social events together. Date rape also occurs among preteens and teens in similar scenarios. In a 1995 study by the University of Wisconsin, Madison, 69 percent of students surveyed had been drinking prior to being raped, and 74 percent said the perpetrator had also been drinking. Victims of date rape are often reluctant to report the crime and delay seeking help—frequently, they aren't even sure if rape occurred or if they were somehow to blame for it happening.

One women's study indicates that 683,000 women are forcibly raped each year, and that 84 percent of rape victims didn't report the offense to the police. From 1992 to 1993, 92 percent of rapes were committed by known assailants. About half of all rapes and sexual assaults against women were committed by friends and acquaintances. And 26 percent were committed by intimate partners.

Christy, a college sophomore, felt she had met the

perfect guy. Mark was charming, attractive, smart, and an outstanding wide receiver on the school's varsity football team. He was a member of one of the most popular fraternities and was basically a well-liked and fun-loving guy. Christy and Mark dated on weekends—usually catching a movie or concert. Mark didn't drink when he was with Christy, but he did drink when he was with his fraternity brothers. The two continued to date over the course of the fall semester, and had a lot of fun together. Mark was respectful—he didn't pressure Christy to have sex and the two agreed to take things slowly.

One Saturday night, Mark invited Christy to a party at his fraternity house, and she accepted. When Christy arrived, she saw a crowd of people dancing, laughing, drinking, and having a good time. Mark greeted her with a beer in his hand. He gave her a bear hug and a kiss on her lips. It was obvious to Christy that he had been drinking, and he offered her a beer, as well. With all of the loud music, drinking, and dancing, Christy got swept up in the scene. She wasn't sure how many drinks she had consumed. But she did notice that Mark was becoming more aggressive—groping her and kissing her as they danced. To cool things down, the two went to an upstairs bedroom where they could be alone and lie down, since both had become somewhat dizzy from the beer. After they made it to the bedroom, Mark moved closer to Christy and put his arm around her neck as they sat on a bed. Before she knew it, he pulled her down onto the bed began fondling her breasts as he lay on top of her. She told him to stop and tried to get up, but he was too strong. She begged him to stop, but he told her to "shut up" and called her derogatory names as he tore her clothes off. As he held her down, he forced her to have intercourse. Christy blacked out, but when she woke up, Mark was gone. She gathered her clothes and ran from the house in tears. Christy struggled to remember what had happened as she lay in the college infirmary. She became so distraught afterward that she dropped out of school and never returned. She never reported the crime to police.

Estimates of violent behavior that takes place in a context of dating or courtship vary because studies and surveys use different methods and definitions of the problem. Some research indicates that the prevalence of dating violence is 9 percent to 65 percent, depending on whether threats and emotional or verbal aggression were included in the definition. The average prevalence among high school students is 22 percent and 32 percent among college students. However, sexual assaults are seldom reported to police.

In one study of more than 1,000 female students at a large urban university, more than 50 percent had experienced some form of unwanted sex—12 percent of these acts were perpetrated by casual dates and 43 percent by steady dating partners. Approximately 80 percent to 95 percent of the rapes that occur on college campuses are committed by someone known to the victim. Approximately 80 percent of male students and 70 percent of female students involved in date rape had been drinking.

Furthermore, the study found that 8 percent of high school girls ages 14 to 17 said a boyfriend or date had forced sex against their will. In another study 40 percent of teenage girls age 14 to 17 reported knowing someone their age who has been beaten by a boyfriend. Experts report that acquaintance rape is especially underreported because women believe that nothing can or will be done and they are unsure how to explain what occurred.

According to a 2000 Milwaukee, Wisconsin, survey conducted as part of a five-year federally funded prevention project called Safe At Home, adolescent girls and boys have a high tolerance for the use of violence in dating relationships. About 33 percent of students surveyed at public and private high schools agreed that violence might be deserved if a girl yelled at her boyfriend or insulted him in front of his friends. Nearly 25 percent said a girl seen talking to another boy might deserve a shove or a slap from her boyfriend.

In one study of students at a large Midwestern university, female respondents reported that 34 percent had experienced unwanted sexual contact, 20 percent had experienced unwanted attempted sexual intercourse, and 10 percent had experienced unwanted intercourse. The majority of incidents were party-related and alcohol use was found to have occurred with more than 75 percent of males and more than 50 percent of females. Conversely, only 9 percent of men reported committing unwanted sexual contact or attempted intercourse and just 3 percent admitted to incidents of unwanted sexual intercourse.

In the mid-1990s, a new phenomenon began to occur involving incidents of date rape. Rapists use illegal drugs to make victims pass out so they are unaware what is happening to them. These "date-rape drugs" include burundanga (a Colombian drug) and ketamine (a veterinary anesthetic), as well as two of the most common—Rohypnol (flunitrazepam) and GHB (gamma hydroxy butyrate).

Rohypnol is much more powerful than other tranquilizers like Valium. It is also called roofies, ruffies, rope, roach, and "the forget pill." It looks like an aspirin tablet. You cannot smell or taste Rohypnol, and it dissolves quickly in liquids. However, Rohypnol's manufacturer, Hoffmann-LaRoche, coats the pills with a dye so the liquid in which the drug is dissolved turns blue. Rohypnol is not approved for use in the United States, but is prescribed in other countries, such as Mexico, to treat sleeping disorders. A small dose can make a person feel, look, and act drunk, whereas a larger dose can render someone unconscious for up to 24 hours. A person usually becomes sleepy within 20 minutes of taking Rohypnol. It can also cause memory

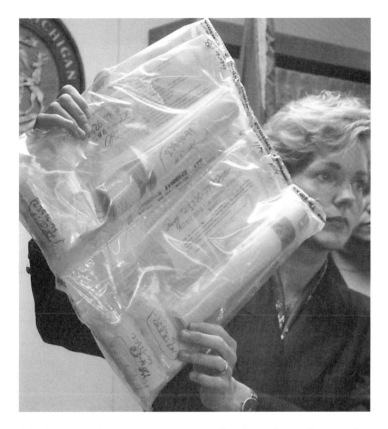

Michigan Attorney General Jennifer Granholm holds an at-home manufacturing kit for the "date rape" drug GHB at a press conference in Detroit in August 1999. After state agents purchased the material needed to make GHB from a Web site, the two men running the business were arrested and charged with manufacturing a controlled substance.

blackouts. The perpetrator usually slips the pill into the victim's beverage (Rohypnol can be deadly when mixed with alcohol). If the victim doesn't pass out, the victim becomes extremely drowsy or incapacitated. At this point, if the victim and perpetrator are in a public place, such as a bar, the perpetrator transports the victim to a secluded location, (a car, a residence) where he rapes her. When the victim awakens, she often has no memory of what has occurred.

GHB, also known as liquid ecstasy, liquid X, grievous bodily harm, liquid E, vita-G, G-juice, or great hormones, is not as common as Rohypnol, but is no less dangerous. Cooked up in bathrooms, kitchens, or street labs, this clear liquid/white powder is a central nervous system depressant, which means it can cause someone to stop breathing. GHB has no smell and it is colorless when dissolved in a liquid. It has a slightly salty taste. Perpetrators usually slip the drug in their victims' drinks or pass it around in a water bottle. GHB causes dizziness, vomiting, nausea, confusion, drowsiness, seizures within 15 minutes, and eventually unconsciousness or coma. Deadly if mixed with alcohol, GHB can cause memory loss.

With date rape drugs, rapists have an easier time committing their crimes because they don't have to use force, threaten, or subdue a victim. The victim is unable to scream if she is unconscious. The victim is unable to remember what happened, which means prosecuting the crime is difficult.

Despite troubling trends like this, within the last two decades, great strides such as a more open discussion of sexual violence, legislative reform, the creation of police and legal units to prosecute offenders, medical and psychological services, and scientific techniques have been made in dealing with crimes of sexual violence. Yet pervasive myths about the crime of rape often discourage victims from legally pursuing their attackers and still allow it to occur with alarming frequency.

Indeed, sex offenses are more difficult to prosecute than other felony crimes, because the victim must recall such painful and intimate events. At one time, a victim had to provide corroboration—independent evidence—of every material element of their sexual assault, including the identity of the perpetrator, the sexual nature of the attack, and the amount of force used. Thus, since it was highly unlikely that there was a witness to a sexual assault, most victims were legally prevented from telling their side of the events to a jury.

And sadly, most women don't report incidents of wife abuse to the police. Some studies indicate the rate of reported incidents to be one in 10. The National Family Violence Survey found that 6.7 percent of assaults on wives are reported to police. Despite changes in social attitudes, many people still consider abuse to be a normal part of life. In addition, women have a difficult time defining themselves as battered; it is an admission of a serious problem that they feel they should be able to handle.

Hedda Nussbaum knew she needed to do something to save her and the two children who lived with her, but felt defenseless against her common-law husband, Joel Steinberg. On November 1, 1987, Steinberg, a Manhattan criminal defense lawyer, beat his six-year-old illegally adopted daughter, Lisa, into a coma. She died four days later. Nussbaum, who was 33 years old and a children's book editor when she met Steinberg, had lived with him for 11 years. She witnessed the child's abuse, however, Nussbaum was a victim of Steinberg's physical and psychological abuse, as well.

Steinberg was exceedingly charming and bright. But even after a few weeks of dating, Nussbaum felt smothered by his constant demands on her time. She stopped dating him. Just a few months later, they reconciled and Nussbaum moved into Steinberg's apartment. Nussbaum made it her mission to be pleasing and acceptable to Steinberg. She even took ballet lessons to become more graceful. The physical abuse started three years later. Nussbaum was injured so badly that she wound up in the emergency room after Steinberg punched her in the eye. Steinberg was unremorseful and unapologetic. Nussbaum was abused more frequently—she suffered a ruptured spleen, bruises and black eyes, and a ripped tear duct. Steinberg forced her to sleep naked on the floor. He forced her to get food from dumpsters, so she was drastically underweight. Yet Nussbaum had convinced herself that she and Steinberg were madly in love and that things would improve. After they adopted Lisa, the violence ceased for several months, but then escalated to new levels, and Lisa became a victim, as well. Others noticed what was going on and tried to

Hedda Nussbaum became a controversial symbol of domestic abuse and its effects on female victims. Her case is an example of the need for intervention by family, friends, and employees from law enforcement, schools, the workplace, medical facilities, and other sectors of society to help prevent and eradicate such horrors of abuse against women.

intervene. Neighbors regularly called the police. When officers arrived on the scene, Steinberg denied anything was wrong. Social workers were summoned, but none followed up. Even Lisa's teachers accepted her made-up explanations for her bruises. Steinberg's hold on Nussbaum was unmistakable. She attempted to leave him no less than five times, but always returned.

After Lisa's death police arrested Nussbaum with Steinberg. Nussbaum was examined by doctors at a hospital. Her wounds were staggering: a ruptured spleen; an ulcerous, gangrenous leg from Steinberg's beatings with a stick; sunken, black eyes; cauliflower ear; a broken, collapsed nose; a swollen, split lip; missing teeth; smashed cheekbones; a splintered jaw; a fractured knee, and numerous cracked ribs. She also had brain damage and psychological damage. Nussbaum spent 13 months in a private psychiatric facility before she was able to function again. Psychiatrists who examined Nussbaum likened her to a hostage or a prisoner of war, robbed of her free will and grasp of reality by a tormentor whose approval had come to mean everything to her. At the time of her arrest, her 16-month-old son, Mitchell, who was also illegally adopted, was returned to his natural mother and Nussbaum never saw him again. Nussbaum was granted immunity for testifying against Steinberg, who was later sentenced to prison for first-degree manslaughter. Today, Nussbaum counsels other domestic violence victims. She encourages these women to have a plan of escape and someplace to go.

Hedda Nussbaum became a controversial symbol of domestic abuse and its effects on female victims. Her case is an example of the need for intervention by family, friends, and employees from law enforcement, schools, the workplace, medical facilities, and other sectors of society to help prevent and eradicate such horrors of abuse against women.

WOMEN'S ROLE IN SOCIETY

Many feminists claim violence against women is the result of a patriarchal culture that encourages and rewards male dominance. In *Against Our Will: Men, Women and Rape*, author Susan Brownmiller details cultural mythologies surrounding rape and images of rape victims going back to biblical times. Patricia Ireland, former president of the National Organization for Women, says violence against women has been accepted throughout history.

Betty Friedan, feminist, and author of "The Feminine Mystique" is the founder of the National Organization for Women. NOW is a women's rights group that supports equality for women in the United States.

In ancient times, in the quest for women, invading clans would kill adult males and enslave women and children. Rape and other forms of physical and psychological violence were used to control women and force them to submit in their new communities. Over time, this violence became characteristic of normal gender relations in society. Examples include male control of women in families, witch burning in 16th century Europe, female genital mutilation in

From ancient times, violent control of women has become characteristic of normal gender relations in society. The Taliban militia has taken control in parts of Afghanistan. They have instituted religious laws that forbid women from attending school, working outside the home, or appearing in public without the traditional Burqa covering.

Africa, bride burning in India, war crimes in Bosnia, and shame killings in the Middle East.

Throughout history, laws have recognized the right and duty of husbands to control and discipline family members, even if it meant killing them. Legalized violence against wives goes back to the late Roman period. In the Middle Ages in Europe, the subservient role of women was well established. In 14th century France, a man could legally beat his wife for failure to obey reasonable commands as long as he didn't kill or permanently maim her.

Between the 16th and 18th centuries, when beatings or floggings were society's accepted method of maintaining law and order, it was only natural that men used violence to maintain law and order in their families. A husband was limited to punches, kicks and whippings, which left no permanent marks. Hitting pregnant women was never condoned, and weapons were forbidden. Only when the use of violence began to be viewed as an unsatisfactory solution to problems did violence against wives begin to be seen as an unacceptable part of marriage. It wasn't until 1829 in England that the husband's right to chastise his wife was taken out of the statutes, although wife abuse has remained a practice until today. Evidence suggests that women had more decision-making power relative to men during the colonial period than during any other period in American history. In 17th century America, women were seen as autonomous sexual beings rather than as objects or possessions of men. Still, rape, domestic violence, and other forms of sexual violence are documented from that time.

In colonial America, the English common law tradition allowing chastisement prevailed with the exception of Puritans, who forbade wife beating, although they hanged witches. The Puritans established the Body of Liberties to reinforce hierarchy within the family and society and to limit illegitimate violence. They sought to protect less powerful members of the family and society only if they were seen as blameless for violence against them, and they sought to punish those who were sinful, stubborn, or disobedient. However, these laws were rarely enforced, and when they were, perpetrators received light sentences. In other colonies, controlling family violence was of little concern. During the postcolonial period, people were more concerned with protecting their families from state intervention than protecting family members from each other.

In the mid-19th century United States, when there were few laws regarding wife abuse or other forms of family violence, a husband's right to beat his wife was gradually eroded by local police and the

In the mid-19th century United States, there were few laws regarding wife abuse or other forms of family violence. Societal and religious mores taught women that it was their religious and ethical duty to yield to the needs and desires of their husbands and it was in their spiritual best interests to "have the badness beaten out of them."

courts. The first major American case of domestic abuse was found in the state supreme court case of *Calvin Bradley v. the State* in Mississippi in 1824. Bradley was convicted in a lower court of assault and battery against his wife with the court ruling that he had gone to excessive lengths to chastise his wife. Wife assault became illegal in legislation passed in Tennessee in 1850 and in Georgia in 1857 the crime became a misdemeanor. Moderate forms of wife beating were declared legal, and more serious forms declared illegal in a series of appellate court decisions that began in Mississippi in 1824 and continued in North Carolina in 1864 and 1868, and other states before 1900.

In 1871, an Alabama court reached a landmark decision that denied the husband's right to physically abuse his wife even moderately or with restraint. Yet while a husband could no longer legally beat his wife, his wife had no legal recourse against her husband. In a landmark case, *Self v. Self*, the Supreme Court of California found that the right to sue "would destroy the peace and harmony of the house."

Societal and religious mores taught women that it was their religious and ethical duty to yield to the needs and desires of their husbands and it was in their spiritual best interests to "have the badness beaten out of them." Only when an appeal to reason or to faith failed was the use of violence justified.

In the 19th century, as the United States evolved from an agrarian economy to an industrialized nation, the social organization of gender in families changed drastically. From the 1700s to the end of the 1800s, men became increasingly associated with wage earning instead of farming. Women became associated with the role of homemaker, which contributed to a decline in their economic and social power relative to men, while men became defined by their work outside of the home. As the United States became more industrialized, violence against women was rationalized, given their status as weak, unintelligent, and unproductive beings. In addition, women became increasingly vulnerable due to the fact that families as social units were now seen as private, intimate, and more self-contained, rather than as extensions of the community at large.

In the antebellum period of the 19th century, the feminist and temperance movements drew public attention to wife beating. Feminists believed that family violence was due to alcohol abuse, and that wives were responsible for attending to their husbands' moral rehabilitation. In the 20th century, wife abuse was perceived as a problem to be contained in families. Society refused to recognize the issue of the patriarchal control of women and ostracized violent families as being abnormal. The battered women's movement didn't take shape until the 1970s, when feminists in England opened a women's center that became a shelter to harbor abused women. The first shelters in the United States were sponsored by Al-Anon, which focused on treating alcoholism as the cause of violent behavior. But the feminist movement helped wife abuse become recognized as a social problem rather than as a personal problem in the 1970s. As a result, services, such as shelters, for abused women became more prevalent as awareness of the problem spread. Foundations, charitable organizations, mental health boards and government agencies all stepped up to the plate financially to support these services.

In 1971, A Woman's Place was founded in Urbana, Illinois, as a refuge for battered women. Another shelter was started in 1974 in St. Paul, Minnesota by a feminist group, Women's Advocates. Other feminist groups formed shelters in the 1970s in Cleveland, Boston, and Ohio. In the 1980s, shelters were founded by the YWCA and other civic organizations. Today, the battered women's movement focuses on finding solutions to the problem within the legal system rather than outside established institutions, such as safe homes and shelters.

Gender relations and expectations are evident in virtually all structures of society, such as schools, families, health care systems, labor markets, political systems, and families. In Western culture, the modern standard of masculinity requires being aggressive, powerful, invulnerable, and able to control others as well as oneself in social situations. This usually implies that a man be athletic, successful financially, and dominant over females. In contrast, the standard of femininity involves nurturing, and emotional, dependent, vulnerable, sexually desirable, and submissive behavior.

Interestingly, these characteristics are idealized,

but not highly valued by American culture. A woman who displays masculine behaviors is somewhat socially acceptable in certain sectors, such as the workplace, but in general women are first and fore-most viewed in the roles of wife, mother, or sexual being. Idealized views of masculinity help spawn gender violence, which is reproduced in the socializa-tion of boys from an early age through the media, schools, families, sports, the military, and politics.

The media dominate popular culture and perpet-uate violence against women. Sex and violence, which are marketed heavily in film, television, advertising, and literature, are dominant components of American culture. Some critics suggest that when sex is depersonalized and made into a commodity, it promotes gender violence by turning women into sex objects. If women are only seen as sex toys, it becomes easier to violate them, and violence is ratio-nalized when depersonalized sexuality is portrayed in music videos, movies, television, and pornographic materials. Perhaps as a consequence, the United States has a higher rate of rape than other countries. Advertisers who use women in advertisements as objects—as body parts—send the message that women aren't human beings.

Feminists point to the fairy tale of *Little Red Riding Hood* as a stereotypical depiction of women. Little Red Riding Hood, a "good" girl, sets out in the woods to bring food to her sick grandmother. The "big, bad wolf" attacks her and a courageous huntsman rescues the frightened girl. The message: Women shouldn't venture into unfamiliar places because they're danger-ous for them; women are vulnerable to being attacked by men and need to be rescued by them (Cinderella and Sleeping Beauty also fall into this category). The fear of crime, especially male violence, perpetuates the image of women as meek, powerless, passive, vul-nerable creatures who are not equal to men, and that they must act and dress a certain way to protect themselves from men. When it comes to rape, the media follow many popular myths: rape is motivated by lust, women provoke rape, and rape is sex. Violence is perceived as being sexy in the media, and through TV, magazines, videos, and other channels, the idea of women as victims is advanced.

In 1970, the President's Commission on Obscenity and Pornography was published. Ever since, a national debate about the effects of sexually explicit materials has ensued. Pornography is a visual or written product that despicts sexual anatomy and or sexual activity designed to promote sexual arousal. Pornographic images are abusive, degrading, or violent to women. Hard-core pornography is usually more detailed in descriptions and visual portrayals of sexual organs and activity, but its most distinguishing feature is the merging of sexual activity with violent acts, such as portrayals of child molestation, rape, sadism, and bestiality. Soft-core porn, such as *Playboy* or *Penthouse* magazines, is believed by many to exploit women through pictures, cartoons, and articles that glorify violence and trivialize incest, child molestation, and rape.

Essentially, the commission found that pornography has no adverse effects. In fact, the report cited two studies from Denmark that claimed sex crimes were down in the country because laws governing pornography were liberalized. However, more current research showed these studies were incomplete and biased, and in the United States studies have shown that arrests for sex offenses increased slightly more than did arrests for nonsex offenses in communities where there was a marked increase in the availability of erotic materials. Many communities, including political groups, feminists, scientists, and investigators, are of the opinion that pornography does contribute to violence against women. A number of major cities

have tried to legally ban pornography on the basis that it is a form of discrimination.

Many feminist groups believe women are portrayed stereotypically in the media, and women have become more concerned with the negative or limiting ways in which they are portrayed. From the feminist point of view, the media depicts violence as exciting and glamorous, which they feel encourages acceptance of violence against women. Certain feminists also believe pornography celebrates, promotes, authorizes and legitimizes rape, sexual harassment, battery, and the abuse of children, all for the sexual pleasure of men.

A 1988 study by the Federal Bureau of Investigation found that 81 percent of violent sexual offenders

Ever since the 1970's, a national debate about the effects of sexually explicit materials has ensued in the United States. Pornography is a visual or written product that depicts sexual anatomy and or sexual activity designed to promote sexual arousal. Soft-core porn is believed by many to exploit women through pictures, cartoons, and articles that glorify violence and trivialize incest, child molestation, and rape.

regularly read or viewed violent pornography. A Michigan State Police study found that porn was viewed just before or during 41 percent of 48,000 sexual crimes committed over 20 years. Serial killer Ted Bundy admitted that pornography played a role in the chain of events that led to his violent behavior and eventual murders. Some believe that hard-core pornography, at its worst, contributes to sexual violence directly. But the adult entertainment industry and others assert that recognizing the link between hard-core porn and violence would permit rapists to go free or avoid taking responsibility for the violent acts they've committed. Still others contend that pornography is an important factor in how men view sexuality and gender relations. To some men who have used pornography and committed sexual violence, pornography was an important factor in shaping a male-dominant view of sexuality. In several cases, the material contributed to their difficulty in separating fantasy from reality. Others simulated violent and abusive sex acts from pornographic material in their own sexual encounters.

In her book, *The Age of Sex Crime*, author Jane Caputi contends that serial sex killers act to enforce misogyny—the hatred of women—in our culture.

"These are not deviants, these are not monsters from nowhere, they're actually performing a cultural function, in enforcing misogyny—the hatred of women—in showing that women are prey, etcetera, and in acting out masculinity in totally dominating the feminine," says Caputi, who discusses women's role as victim in the landmark documentary film *No Safe Place: Violence Against Women* produced by public television station KUED in Salt Lake City, Utah. "[Popular culture] makes [rape] glamorous, it eroticizes that kind of violence against women and makes it appear consensual, as if women seek this out and want it. *Gone With the Wind* is, of course, classic

in that we see a scene of marital rape and the woman is made to smile as if seeming to enjoy it."

In the film, Caputi adds, "There's ads for jeans in which women are shown licking the floor. That's a common technique in domestic violence, not just hitting the woman but humiliating her, either through words or through making her perform demeaning acts."

At one time, turning to the judicial system for help was unlikely to result in assistance for the victim of spousal abuse. Wife abuse was viewed as a matter to be resolved within the family. In 1991, only 17 states kept data on reported domestic violence offenses.

Many feminist groups believe women are portrayed stereotypically in the media, and women have become more concerned with the negative ways in which they are portrayed. In 1995, Calvin Klein was investigated over alleged exploitation in advertising materials.

Many legal authorities believed a wife was responsible for her own beating by inciting the husband to lose his temper. Insensitive and unresponsive treatment by police, prosecutors, and judges often resulted in low reporting and conviction rates. Alcohol and drug abuse were considered the basis of the problem, and so legal authorities urged treatment of alcoholism to end the abuse. Moreover, it was thought that it was a wife's duty to accept the abuse as part of her marital fate. Today, a victim is far more likely to have her complaint handled seriously and to have the abuse she suffered considered a crime.

It is common knowledge that police officers dislike domestic calls and don't always provide support to women, sometimes sympathizing with abusers. In the mid-1960s, Detroit police dispatchers were instructed to screen out family disturbance calls unless they suspected "excessive" violence. Officers were taught to avoid making an arrest at all costs.

Police officers often try to dissuade victims from filing charges. Prosecutors are often reluctant to prosecute domestic violence cases. They feel women frequently drop charges after a short time and that the prosecutor's time spent has been wasted. Judges rarely impose the maximum sentence on convicted abusers, who most often receive a fine or probation.

In the past, the desire to maintain the family unit meant that many judges were reluctant to punish batterers. One report cited a judge who claimed, "Even if the woman shows up in my court with visible injuries, I don't really have any way of knowing who's responsible or who I should kick out of the house. Yes, he may have beaten her, but nagging and a sharp tongue can be just as bad. Maybe she used her sharp tongue so often that she provoked him to hit her."

And despite the use of injunctions, there is little to prevent a husband who has been arrested and then released from returning and beating up the victim

again. In fact, in order to prove that he still controls
the power in the relationship, he may return with
greater violence than ever before. The number of
houses and shelters available for women to flee to
safety is still limited despite an increase in the number
of institutions. Medical authorities at hospitals and
doctor's offices are often unsympathetic or resist getting involved and are reluctant to follow through with
abuse cases.

3

MYTHS VS. REALITY

Many myths about domestic violence and rape are perpetuated through the acceptance of gender-role stereotyping and the media's depiction of women, sex, and violence. As a result, women are often seen as being responsible for their victimization: they deserved their fate, they were asking for it, and somehow they are to blame for their circumstances.

Much needs to be done to educate people about the truths and realities of domestic violence and rape. Through more accurate and balanced depictions of men and women in the media, movies, advertising, and books, women and men can gain a better understanding of human relationships and

---

Many myths about domestic violence and rape are perpetuated through the acceptance of gender-role stereotyping and the media's depiction of women, sex, and violence. As a result, women are often seen as being responsible for their victimization.

help to reduce the incidence of rape and domestic violence.

Indeed, an examination of statistics clarifies the truths about rape and domestic violence. Many people believe that domestic violence occurs only in lower income households, yet a review of reports from police records, victim services, and academic studies shows otherwise. Domestic violence exists equally in every socioeconomic group, regardless of race or culture. However, women in families with incomes below $10,000 are more likely than women with higher incomes to be victims of violence by a domestic partner, according to the National Crime Victimization Survey. In addition, nearly 1 million incidents of domestic violence occurred each year from 1992 to 1996 and 85 percent of victims were women.

While alcohol and drug abuse often play a role in domestic violence, they are not the root causes of violence in the home. According to the National Crime Prevention Council, because male batterers also abuse alcohol and other drugs, it's easy to conclude that these substances may cause domestic violence. They do increase the lethality of the violence. But they also offer the batterer another excuse to evade responsibility for their behavior. An abusive male typically controls his actions, even when under the influence of drugs or alcohol, by choosing a time and place for the assaults to take place in private. Moreover, successful completion of a drug treatment program doesn't guarantee an end to battering. Domestic violence and substance abuse are two different problems that should be treated separately.

It would be wrong to assume that battered women don't leave because they enjoy being hit. The unfortunate answer is that many battered women simply have no place to go or no one to turn to. Moreover, a battered woman may put herself in greater danger by leaving an abusive partner who has the wherewithal to track her down, especially if she takes children with her. It is not unusual for an abusive man to demand custody of a child as a way to retain power and control over the woman.

Rebecca wanted desperately to leave David, but she was not financially able to do so. David insisted that she stay at home to raise their two children, while he enjoyed a successful career as a hospital administrator. Whenever David thought Rebecca might be leaving, he told her that he would use his resources to hire an attorney to divorce her and seek full custody of their kids. He said she would be left with nothing when he was through with her.

Women in Rebecca's situation are often unwilling to leave their children behind, and yet are unable to pay for rent, day care, health insurance, and other basic expenses if they do leave their abusive partner. They often have few financial resources to support themselves and their children (on average, a woman earns slightly more than half of what a man earns). Shelters provided by government agencies, foundations, mental health boards, and civic organizations are usually filled to capacity. At least 70 percent of all battered women seeking shelter have children who accompany them and 17 percent bring three or more children By the early 1980s, shelters in the U.S. were serving about 270,000 women and children annually. Often battered women cannot lean on family, friends, or coworkers for support. Battered women fear retaliation for leaving, harassment, and further violence from the abuser. Statistically, the most dangerous time for a battered woman is when she is leaving or he believes she is leaving.

Domestic abuse is not a private, family matter. It is a crime and a social problem that affects as many as 50 percent of all U.S. women. Violence against wives will occur at least once in 66 percent of all marriages; at least 25 percent of wives are beaten during their marriage. More than 1 million abused women seek medical help for injuries and 20 percent of visits by women to emergency medical services are caused by battering.

The National Crime Victimization Survey says that domestic violence results in financial losses to women victims conservatively estimated to be $150 million per year (at least 40 percent for medical expenses, 44 percent for property losses, and the remainder for lost pay). Domestic violence leads to 28,700 emergency room visits per year, 39,000 physician office visits, $44 million in total annual medical costs, and 175,000 lost days of work.

One of the most common myths is that women provoke rape by their behavior, such as going out alone at night, using drugs or alcohol, or wearing tight or low-cut clothes. None of these behaviors justify rape or assault. Contrary to popular belief, rape doesn't only happen to attractive, promiscuous, young women. Anyone can be sexually assaulted (1 out of 10 men are victims of adult sexual assault). Studies show victims include infants, the elderly, lesbians and gays, people with disabilities, and those of every racial, ethnic, religious, economic, and social background. In 1996, 71 out of 100,000 females reported being raped, according to FBI reports. By some estimates, one out of three women will be victims of sexual assault in her lifetime.

Police and government studies have also supported the fact that a woman's attire or behavior doesn't cause rape. Offenders, not victims, must be held accountable for these crimes. According to

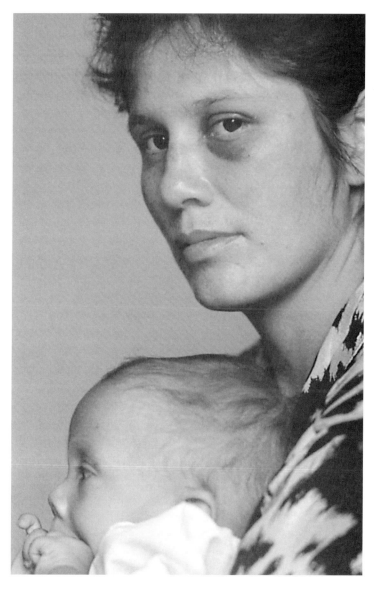

The National Crime Victimization Survey says that domestic violence results in financial losses to women victims conservatively estimated to be $150 million per year (at least 40 percent for medical expenses, 44 percent for property losses, and the remainder for lost pay). Domestic violence leads to 28,700 emergency room visits per year, 39,000 physician office visits, $44 million in total annual medical costs, and 175,000 lost days of work.

Mary Dickson, writer and coproducer of a PBS documentary on rape, *No Safe Place: Violence Against Women*, rapists are aggressive and have problems controlling their anger. They often have distorted views about women and sex. Many have a mixed criminal history and a pattern of victimizing people.

Another popular belief—that most sexual assaults are committed by strangers at night in dark, isolated places—is false. According to the National Crime Victimization Survey, from 1992 to 1993, 92 percent of rapes of women were committed by someone familiar to the victim. About 50 percent of all rapes and sexual assaults against women are committed by friends or acquaintances, and 26 percent by a partner. More than 50 percent of sexual assaults occur in the home, and just as many happen during daylight hours as at night.

C. Y. Roby is the former director of Intermountain Specialized Abuse Treatment Center in Salt Lake City, Utah, which began, in 1983, providing treatment for sexual abuse for victims and perpetrators and also treats domestic violence. He said:

> We have a tendency to promote that kind of stereotype [that when most people think of rape, they think of a stranger attacking an unknown woman] especially through the media... you see a picture or a scene of a park and then some individual leaps out, or it's a dark alley. That's so much less common than other forms of rape, that we have a tendency to look on it and then say, well in order to keep safe, what I need to do then is stay out of the park at night, stay out of the dark alleys at night and I won't end up being raped. And yet, the vast majority of rapists are known to the victim. It typically is in the context of a date situation... and there usually is some kind of an acquaintanceship relationship between the victim and the perpetrator.

"We want to feel safe so we want to believe that rapists have a particular profile in terms of they're easy to identify—they wear trench coats, they live under the viaduct or hang out in vacant buildings and have crazed looks in their eyes," said Abby Maestas, executive director of the Rape Recovery Center in Salt Lake City, Utah, in the documentary film *No Safe Place*. "And that's not true. What we have found through the clients that are served at the Rape Recovery Center is that a rapist can be anyone —a father, a grandfather, an uncle, a neighbor, a brother, a son."

WHAT CAUSES AGGRESSIVE BEHAVIOR?

At least three out of every 100 men in the United States, or 1.8 million, severely assault their female partners or girl-friends each year. Such assaults include punching, kicking, choking, threats of violence with a knife or gun, or use of a knife or gun. What drives some-one to commit violence against women?

In 1992, Donna Manion, who lived in Winches-ter, Massachusetts, visited the local police station where she took out a restraining order against her ex-boyfriend, Ernest C. Anthony Jr., Donna didn't know that Ernest was a convicted felon. He had a 10-year history of violent crime and had previously ignored at least two restraining orders filed by women he had abused years before. For several years, Donna and Ernest had an abusive relationship, but Donna thought she could change him. She finally gave up and ended the relationship. After Ernest smashed the windows of her car, Donna went to the police for help. That same day, Ernest put a gun to the head of Donna's mother, Gertrude Manion, and killed her in her driveway. He then kidnapped Donna and drove her across the country, only to return to Massachusetts, where he held police at bay for nearly 10 hours before killing himself at his neighbor's house. Donna was rescued unharmed by police.

At least three out of every 100 men in the United States, or 1.8 million, severely assault their female partners or girlfriends each year. Such assaults include punching, kicking, choking, threats of violence with a knife or gun, or use of a knife or gun. What drives someone to commit violence against women? Researchers have identified two types of batterers. One category includes criminal types who have engaged in antisocial behavior since adolescence. They are hedonistic, charismatic, and impulsive, and have a history of physical and emotional abuse of others. They beat their wives and abuse them emotionally to stop them from interfering with their own need to get what they want when they want it. Although they may say that they are sorry after a beating and beg for forgiveness, they are usually not sorry. They feel entitled to whatever they want whenever they want it, and try to get it by whatever means necessary. Some of them are psychopaths—they lack a conscience and are incapable of feeling remorse or empathy. They don't experience sadness and rarely experience fear, unless it is over something that is about to happen to them. They are incapable of forming intimate relationships. Their partners serve as sources of gratification—sex, economic benefits, social status. They don't fear abandonment and won't be controlled. They often come from abusive families that were devoid of love and security. They are likely to abuse drugs and alcohol. They are often dependent financially on their wives. These batterers are motivated by the desire to get as much immediate gratification as possible. They retaliate quickly and violently when they feel threatened—and can target anyone from a partner to a coworker. It is very difficult for women who are battered by these men to leave. It usually takes a long time because these men are so violent and impulsive. They act without remorse or a conscience and are unsympathetic. However, if a woman does manage to escape, this type of batterer is less likely to pursue the battered woman after her escape—he merely finds a new victim. He isn't interested in being "tied down" emotionally and is not as obsessive as the other type of batterer.

Martin was able to easily intimidate Carrie and keep her under his thumb. He was a master of sweet talking women while also conveying that he was not one to be messed with. He was able to manipulate women (and most anybody) into believing that he was smart, ambitious, moral, and decent—the consummate con artist. He knew that Carrie was vulnerable and preyed on this. When they were dating, he knew that she desperately wanted to meet someone, fall in love, get married, and have children. This was the perfect life to her. So he made her believe that he was the "perfect" guy. Martin took delight in degrading and insulting Carrie by calling her names. Although Carrie often tried to defend herself, she was no match for Martin's rage. He didn't hesitate to beat, scream, and yell at her in front of their three-year-old son. Martin wanted to be able to do whatever he wanted whenever he wanted, and no woman of his was going to tell him what to do or control him. Verbally and physically abusing Carrie was Martin's way of keeping her in line.

The second type includes batterers who are more likely to confine their violence to family members, especially wives or girlfriends. They typically feel that battering women is acceptable because they more than likely witnessed this scenario growing up in their parents' household. They are not as likely to have been antisocial as adolescents. These men are emotionally dependent on their wives—they are prone to fits of jealous rage and have a fear of abandonment.

O. J. Simpson was emotionally dependent on Nicole Brown Simpson. He was jealous and possessive and didn't display violence outside the relationship. Even after Simpson started dating another woman, he continued to stalk his former wife.

These feelings of jealousy can border on paranoia, with these batterers imagining and accusing their partners of having affairs. They take extra steps to suppress the independence of their partners. Their need for control stems from their fear of abandonment. These batterers target their aggression on family members—usually their partners—and can be unrelenting and obsessive.

O. J. Simpson was emotionally dependent on Nicole Brown Simpson. He was jealous and possessive and didn't display violence outside the relationship. Even after Simpson started dating another woman, Paula Barbieri, after their divorce, he continued to stalk Nicole Brown Simpson. There are accounts that Barbieri ended her relationship with Simpson because of his obsession with his former wife; coincidently this was the same day Nicole Brown Simpson was murdered.

It is easier to leave this type of batterer, but he is more likely to stalk and continue to abuse or even murder the battered woman after her escape. He is also more likely to become obsessed with the battered woman after her escape—even years later. Adults who grew up in a violent home are more likely to become abusers or victims of domestic violence. As a result of this violent environment, they may see abuse as a "normal" way of life.

Allen Amir grew up in a Boston suburb where he was raised by his mother and stepfather, who both had violent tendencies. Throughout his life Allen witnessed violence against his mother and saw its impact on his friends. All the signs of abuse were evident in his home—belittling behavior, economic control, verbal threats, and actual physical assault. He saw guns, knives, and an ax wielded at his mother. One time, he saw two men engaged in a bloody knife fight over her. For years, Allen feared getting married and having children because he thought he might resort to violence against loved ones. This fear haunted his relationships with women. Once while talking to a female friend, he began to think that he was a monster. But he realized he didn't have to continue the cycle of violence. He joined a peer group and eventually married. He now heads a program focused on educating schoolchildren about domestic violence.

In abusive relationships, the abuser may use a variety of tactics other than physical violence to maintain power and control over his partner. Survivors of domestic violence are often subject to "emotional violence," such as put-downs, public humiliation, name-calling, mind games, and manipulations by their partners. It is common for abusers to be extremely jealous and forbid their victims to see friends and family. Batterers often use threats of violence, suicide, or of taking away children.

Michael Kimmel, a sociologist at the State University of New York at Stony Brook, has received international recognition for his work on men and masculinity. He says men tend to be violent against women when they feel their power eroding. Kimmel says that these men have clung to the traditional model of masculinity while others have realized that this model no longer works in society. They seek revenge on those whom they believe are compromising their masculinity—women. In the film *No Safe Place*, Kimmel said:

> Well, the basic rules of manhood, if I were to put them this way, are no sissy stuff, that's the first rule. You can never do anything that even remotely hints of femininity. The second rule is, be a big wheel. You know, we measure masculinity by the size of your check, wealth, power, status, things like that. The third rule is, be a sturdy oak. You show that you're a man by not ever showing your emotions. And the fourth rule is, give 'em hell. Always go forward, exude an aura of daring and aggression in everything that you do. And this model of masculinity has been around for an awfully long time.

Studies have shown that sexually violent perpetrators share many common risk factors. Rapists often have had early sexual experiences (both forced and voluntary), adhere to sex-role stereotyping, have

negative attitudes toward women, consume alcohol, and accept many rape myths. Men who have a family history of observing or experiencing abuse are more likely to inflict abuse and violence on others and be more sexually aggressive.

Perpetrators of dating violence have been found to have sexually aggressive peers, indulge in heavy alcohol or drug use (or both), accept the idea of dating violence, and assume key roles in dating (such as initiating the date, being the driver, and paying

In abusive relationships, the abuser may use a variety of tactics other than physical violence to maintain power and control over his partner. Survivors of domestic violence are often subject to "emotional violence," such as put-downs, public humiliation, name-calling, mind games, and manipulations by their partners. Batterers often use threats of violence, suicide, or of taking away children.

dating expenses). Studies show that date rapists also have engaged in previous sexual intimacy with the victim, have a history of interpersonal violence, believe in traditional sex roles, maintain adversarial attitudes about relationships and rape myths, and miscommunicate about sex. "For many of the individuals that I worked with, once an individual accepted a date, the way they looked at it, she was also accepting to go to bed with them," says C.Y. Roby, director of Intermountain Specialized Abuse Treatment Center, "They would talk to me about the fact that, 'Well, she agreed to go out with me, so wasn't she really agreeing to have a sexual relationship with me?' "

Dr. Michael Ghiglieri, an Arizona-based biological anthropologist who has written extensively about male violence, says testosterone is responsible for male traits, including violence. "Testosterone actually forces aggressive behavior. The fact is, testosterone does affect human male attitudes and the propensities to violence," says Ghiglieri. In the film *No Safe Place*, he says, "Violence is a male tactic. But I think in general if you want to get the simplest perspective on it, males use violence to control females and they do it very often, and they control those females for sexual reasons."

Jane Caputi, author of *The Age of Sex Crime*, says that to look at male violence from a biological perspective is skewed and nothing more than "scientific sexism." In the film *No Safe Place*, Kimmel says, "We might see men initiating aggression against women, we might see men acting against women, but the men themselves don't experience it that way. They experience it as revenge or retaliation. I mean, just listen for a minute to the way in which we describe women's beauty and sexuality. We describe it as a violence against us. She is a knockout, a bombshell, dressed to kill, a femme fatale, stunning, ravishing. I mean all of these are words of violence against us."

Still, rape also has been viewed as a crime of control and violence and not one of a purely sexual nature. "Males often grow up and realize that the way to get what they want when they're younger is through aggressive means. So, it's something that we talk negatively about, but we quietly, I think, condone it and actually seem to promote it," says Roby in *No Safe Place*.

Yet others would argue that issues of control and dominance cannot be separated from the fact that rape is, in nature, a crime of sex, and that control and power are used as the mechanism to gain sex. Says Caputi in *No Safe Place:*

> I think it's really specious to separate violence and sex. I would disagree with some of the early feminists who would say rape is a crime of violence, not a crime of sex. Because, unfortunately, in this culture, sex is completely

Signs of a Potentially Violent Man

- Has history of violent family upbringing
- Tends to use force or violence to solve problems, overreacts to little problems and frustrations, punches walls or throws objects, shows cruelty toward animals
- Abuses alcohol or other drugs
- Has poor sense of self, guards his masculinity by trying to act tough
- Has strong traditional ideas about a man's role and a woman's role in society
- Is jealous of wife or girlfriend, her friends, or family
- Plays with guns, knives, or other deadly objects; threatens to use them to hurt others
- Becomes angry if wife or girlfriend doesn't follow his orders or anticipate his needs
- Experiences extreme emotional high and low moods
- Instills fear and intimidation in wife or girlfriend when angry
- Abuses female acquaintances he dates

Dr. Susan Hanks, former director of the Family and Violence Institute in Alameda, California, says that men beat their wives or girlfriends because they are dependent on women and feel threatened by the notion of them acting or thinking on their own. When a woman is on the verge of leaving an abusive relationship, she is particularly at risk because the abuser is most psychologically vulnerable and feels most rejected.

interfused with violence, with notions of dominance and subordination. As I said, I believe our gender roles are constructed so we have these two constructed genders—masculine and feminine—that are defined by one being powerful and one being powerless. And so therefore powerlessness and power themselves become eroticized.

Dr. Susan Hanks, former director of the Family and Violence Institute in Alameda, California, says that men beat their wives or girlfriends because they are dependent on women and feel threatened by the notion of them acting or thinking on their own. When a woman is on the verge of leaving an abusive relationship, she is particularly at risk because the abuser is most psychologically vulnerable and feels most rejected, says Dr. Hanks. The abuser deals with these feelings by acting violently towards the woman who he perceives is causing them.

ABUSERS: TREATMENT AND INTERVENTION

Charles was a manipulative man who knew when he had pushed his wife over the edge. He abused his wife, Connie, all through their five-year marriage. Anything would set him off. Connie recognized the signs when a beating was to come. Controlling Connie made Charles feel powerful. He verbally abused her and tracked her every move. She was given a set amount of time to run errands whenever she left the house. If she was even five minutes late, she was beaten. Connie tried to do what Charles said and comply to his wishes, lest she suffer another beating. After the beatings, he would apologize, give her gifts, and express his affection. But he was extremely intimidating—his very presence made Connie tremble

Group discussions help batterers to learn relaxation techniques and to learn to recognize anger warning signs, how to temper their anger, how to communicate with their partners, and how to avoid unnecessary conflicts. Court-mandated treatment programs help batterers own up to misdeeds and take responsibility for their actions.

in fear. Charles isolated Connie from her friends and family to keep her from telling them about the abuse. To make matters worse, Charles drank, which brought on his anger. Connie lived in fear and was too afraid to tell anyone about her abuse for fear of being killed by Charles. Connie even contemplated killing Charles to end her misery. Fortunately, Connie didn't have to take such extreme measures.

Police officers convinced her to press charges after they spotted her in a local restaurant with bruises on her face. Charles received a sentence of 18 months in jail. After six months, he was released from an intensive alcohol program under the condition that he enroll in a treatment program for batterers. Charles complied because he was intent on changing his ways. As a first step in the group, Charles had to own up to his misdeeds with the goal of taking responsibility for his actions. It took Charles four weeks to accept his violent actions. Usually it takes several months for batterers to own up to their battering—they blame everyone else from the police to their partners. Some never get past this step and go back to jail. In the next phase, Charles focused on learning why he battered and how to control his anger. This included group discussions about their childhood experiences, their parents' behavior toward one another, and their own attitudes and ways of communicating. Charles was uncomfortable sharing his feelings with the other men, but he wanted to get help so he could return to his family. The batterers also learned relaxation techniques, how to recognize anger warning signs, how to temper their anger, how to communicate with their partners, and how to avoid unnecessary conflicts. Charles and the other batterers also listened to battered women from a local women's center to gain insight into their perspective. Charles was mortified by what he heard.

For Charles, the group discussions and alcohol programs helped him to turn his life around. He was able to improve his relationship with Connie and gained a new sense of respect for her. He stopped drinking, learned to control his temper, and learned to allow his wife to do things (like go back to school) and to make decisions for their family. Whenever he feels his anger rising, he takes a "time out" and discusses things rationally with Connie. He has learned to listen to her point of view. Charles says he has changed for the better and is focused on making things better for good.

Batterer intervention programs, which started in the mid-1970s, are the major alternative to jail for male abusers. These programs are designed to stop the violence by treating the abusive husband or boyfriend. One study found that batterers who were referred to such programs by judges, social workers, or wives or who attended on their own initiative were most likely to complete them. Many batterers who would be unlikely to enroll themselves in a program on their own are forced by the court to complete the course, with the hope that this education would lessen the likelihood of violence reoccurring.

Batterers can abuse their partners even when they aren't being physically violent by using verbal or emotional abuse. Virtually all batterers also abuse their wives emotionally with verbal threats, use intimidating actions such as the destruction of pets or property, direct humiliating and degrading remarks toward their partners, and attempt to rob their partners of their autonomy as human beings. Once a woman has been battered and violence has been established as a method of control, emotional abuse can be especially frightening and controlling. Emotional abuse can come to serve the same controlling function that physical abuse does. Battering is physical aggression with a purpose: to control, intimidate, and subjugate another human being. Fear is the force that provides battering with its power. Injuries help sustain the fear. Batterers are unable to accept any influence from women. They have a desire to assert their authority, to teach their wives a lesson. They are outraged when women call them on their violent behavior. They often become more aggressive when women assert themselves. Then the emotional abuse starts.

Voluntary participants in treatment programs usually have been motivated to enter the program to prevent the girlfriend or wife from leaving or to get her to come back. In other words, the woman assumes the burden of forcing the man into treatment. But when the violence issues have been resolved, either by the woman returning or leaving, the man is much less likely to be motivated to complete the programs.

"Group therapy is a way for men to open up and talk about their own abuse and relationships with women," said Gerald Evans, director of The Men's Resources Center in Wayne, Pennsylvania, which treats men going through divorce and provides counseling through individual and group therapy. "Over the years, men isolate themselves, keeping their pain, vulnerability, and secrets to themselves." Most of the clients at the center have never been in a group before, and most cannot talk openly about their emotions. Usually the only person they can talk to is their wife or girlfriend, but many do not feel heard and are dissatisfied with the level of communication.

Evans adds that with abusers, there is a very fine line between what behavior is acceptable and what is considered "wimpish." They have a hard time creating intimacy for themselves. After the first act of abuse, they often feel a sense of relief, because this is how they express themselves. This feeling is replaced with the fear that they will lose the victim because they believe they can't live without her and need to feel they can control her.

"Most of these men can't imagine being without someone," said Evans. "They can't be independent to make decisions. They get defensive if they feel

unappreciated or undesirable and get angry in attempts to scare the victim so she will settle down and back off. When she doesn't back off, the violence occurs."

A study of court-mandated programs found that they offer promise for the reform of abusive men through education or rehabilitation. Many batterers who are forced to attend such programs may improve their behavior, but these treatments can vary widely and produce minimal effectiveness. Techniques used in treatment include anger control, anger journals, relaxation, role-playing, increasing self-esteem, and changing attitudes toward traditional sex roles.

Coordinated Community Response (CCR) is widely used among certified treatment programs for batterers. However, CCR has not been proven to be

Tootie Welker holds up a booklet used in the treatment of domestic violence offenders. She was speaking as a proponent of House bill 313 that would revise Montana domestic violence laws. A study of court-mandated programs found that many batterers who are forced to attend such programs may improve their behavior.

effective in reducing battering. CCR relies on community organization and links together the criminal justice system, advocacy work, and the education of batterers. CCR involves the coordinated efforts of education groups for batterers, support groups for battered women, shelters, police practices, and prosecutorial tendencies. The best CCR programs also include probation officers and judges. All parties involved believe that in order for violence to stop, batterers must be held accountable.

For example, instead of police officers blaming the battered woman, police actions support the view that the batterer is solely responsible for the violence. If the batterer is part of an education program with a CCR philosophy, probation officers punish him for not showing up for group education sessions by making sure he goes to jail. Education of batterers usually involves working in groups. The emphasis is on trying to get batterers to accept responsibility for the violence without blaming their partners and changing the attitudes of batterers so that they no longer see violence as an acceptable response in any situation. An emphasis is made of the connection between battering and our patriarchal culture, which has designed marriage as an institution that benefits men and oppresses women. The ways in which batterers wield power and control, through emotional and physical abuse, are discussed. Treating batterers in groups allows them to confront one another regarding their tendency to minimize, deny, and distort their abuse. The power of being confronted by another batterer is often much greater than a similar confrontation coming from a counselor.

Treatment programs that teach batterers to control their anger and improve their social skills have fallen into disfavor in recent years among much of the advocacy community, which believes that batterers don't batter because they are angry, but to achieve instrumental goals such as power and control. Most of the negative feelings about these programs are based on political ideology rather than objective evidence regarding the effectiveness of these programs. Some doctors have begun to experiment with drugs such as Paxil, Prozac, and Zoloft to treat batterers. These drugs are collectively known as Selective Serotonin Reuptake Inhibitors (SSRIs). They increase the supply of serotonin in the brain. Serotonin is a chemical that aids in the transmission of information from one nerve cell to another. It has been shown that low rates of serotonin are related to impulsive aggression in animals and to impulsive violence in humans. These drugs are being investigated in terms of their effectiveness at curbing violence.

SSRIs may be helpful for highly impulsive batterers and those who are prone to fits of rage. These drugs are also effective antidepressants, as some batterers have histories of depression. However, some advocates are concerned that if batterers are given drugs, they are perceived as being ill, and therefore not responsible for their behavior. Furthermore, their being ill could be used as a defense strategy in criminal court.

A popular form of court referral is the pretrial diversion, in which charges are dismissed if the batterer completes a battering intervention program. But evidence suggests there can be significant problems with inappropriate referrals, the inability to punish those who fail to complete required sessions, and the use of unqualified programs.

One study, which evaluated 30 programs, found that half were considered model programs (they had provided more than five years of full-time counseling, were involved in training, and had evaluated their program outcomes). Of all programs, 25 percent included some form of anger control treatment; 20 percent emphasized issues of power and control, in addition to other techniques such as relaxation, assertiveness, communication, and responsibility skills. Program lengths varied from less than three months to seven months or more. Nearly 50 percent of the programs reported participant completion rates of 50 percent or less, although 38 percent reported rates of 75 percent or more.

Batterer intervention programs use primarily three theoretical approaches to stop violence. The society and culture approach attributes battering to social and cultural norms and values that endorse the use of violence by men against female partners. One feminist model seeks to educate men concerning the impact of these social norms and values, and attempts to resocialize men through education that emphasizes nonviolence and equality in relationships.

The family approach espouses theories of domestic violence focused on the structure and social isolation of families. The family systems' model of intervention focuses on improving communication skills between husband and wife, sometimes with couples counseling, with the goal of family preservation.

The individual approach employs psychological theories attributing domestic violence to personality disorders, the batterer's social environment during childhood, or biological predispositions. Psychotherapeutic interventions target individual problems or build cognitive skills, or both, to help the batterer control violent behaviors.

There is little evidence to suggest that one treatment approach is more effective than another or that one is more effective with a certain type of batterer over another. Despite this, many states have developed standards, or are in the process of developing standards, for the conduct of these programs. Currently, 25 states have county or state standards, or both, five states have drafted standards, and 13 states and the District of Columbia are developing standards.

Confronting abusers with the consequences of their

behavior increases the chance their families will survive and recover, says Im Jung Kwuon, who has counseled male batterers in Los Angeles. Kwuon believes that no one is safe until every batterer is held accountable for his behavior. According to Kwuon, men rarely admit to beating their girlfriends or wives. Most feel justified in their actions because their partners provoked them. According to Kwuon, male batterers can begin the recovery process when they can learn how to express anger without intimidating others around them and when they are able to discuss their childhood memories of witnessing abuse or being abused. But not all participants are treated successfully.

Kwuon recalled a client who had attended numerous classes and had reassured her and others in the group that he and his girlfriend were working things out. However, eventually the client stopped attending classes. Two months later he shot and killed his girlfriend, who was also the mother of his two young sons. Court-ordered counseling is beneficial, says Kwuon, because batterers can learn how to become safer husbands, boyfriends, and fathers. Moreover, she believes that a criminal charge and mandatory anger management classes encourage a batterer to relinquish violence and intimidation to control the women in his life.

Research findings are mixed regarding the effectiveness of police arrest policies as a deterrent to domestic violence. Some studies have reported that police arrests do effectively deter domestic violence when compared with other strategies such as counseling or short separation. Other studies, however, have failed to replicate these findings. Additional studies have suggested that the deterrent effects of arrest may vary depending on factors such as length of time in police custody and the characteristics of the individual arrested.

According to Judith S. Kaye, chief judge of the New York State Court of Appeals, judicial responses

According to Judith S. Kaye, chief judge of the New York State Court of Appeals, judicial responses to cases involving domestic violence are rooted in the past. She says that traditional approaches to such cases often result in battered wives being beaten again when they return home after obtaining a protective order. Procedures are followed, but the underlying problem isn't being solved. However, judges across the country are beginning to make positive, effective changes by becoming active problem-solvers.

to cases involving domestic violence are rooted in the past. She says that traditional approaches to such cases often result in battered wives being beaten again when they return home after obtaining a protective order. Procedures are followed, but the underlying problem isn't being solved. But judges across the country are beginning to make positive, effective changes by becoming active problem-solvers. In New York, for example, there are six domestic violence courts that put an emphasis on victim safety and accountability of defendants. But collaborations with government agencies and community groups are key, says Kaye.

In contrast with treatment of batterers, successful

programs for men involved in crimes such as rape
have been more difficult to develop. Dr. Ron Sanchez,
a psychologist who works with sex offenders in the
Utah State Prison system, says many rapists tend to be
compulsive and repetitive, which makes it difficult to
treat them. They often start the cycle of violence by
becoming voyeurs. Their voyeurism often leads to
burglarizing of homes at night. This behavior escalates
to entertaining fantasies about rape and then eventually
planning and committing rape.

Men rape because it makes them feel powerful and
they want to humiliate another person. They are
aroused by their behavior. For many males, raping a
woman is a way to prove their masculinity. Forcing sex
on another person—whether it be a stranger, a girlfriend, or a wife—is a way to show how macho they are.
Rapists commit crimes of opportunity (a male may be
robbing a home, encounter a woman, and decide to
rape her). Some rapists have mental disabilities that
make them unable to control their behavior (a male
sees a women who he is attracted to and decides to force
sex on her).

A study by the American Psychological Association
found no evidence that the rate of recidivism for treated
rapists was any lower than it was for offenders who
received no treatment. In *No Safe Place*, Sanchez says,
"I think that [you] know we need to be realistic about
what therapy can do. When we talk about treatment,
we're not talking about a disease or an illness that we
can cure with an antibiotic or something like that. It
boils down to a personal choice."

Most reports of rape never result in an arrest. The
FBI estimated that 62 percent of the reported rape cases
never result in the apprehension of the alleged perpetrator, and 98 percent of victims never see their attacker
arrested, tried, convicted, and imprisoned. The nine out
of 10 rape cases that do not result in conviction are
the result of dismissal rather than acquittal. Almost

25 percent of convicted rapists never go to prison; another 25 percent receive sentences in local jails, where the average sentence is 11 months.

In the past, many jurisdictions excluded marital rape from their definition of rape because it wasn't believed a woman could be raped by her husband. After all, a woman was considered the property of her husband and sex was part of her marital obligation. Often marital rapists weren't prosecuted because it was thought that it didn't promote "domestic harmony." This is not the case today, for the most part. Most jurisdictions don't exclude marital rape in their statutes and men have been prosecuted for this offense. However, convictions are difficult to obtain unless there is other evidence of violence or the couple is no longer together.

In *No Safe Place*, Kimmel says:

> I think the trick is we need very strong laws with uncompromising enforcement and all the way through the legal system so that we make it clear as a culture that we won't stand for this. ... We take away all the incentives, all the possibilities, we make it clear this is not okay in this culture. If we as men make it very clear to the women in our lives that we don't support men's violence against women, that we are actively opposed to it, that we are willing to confront other men who we see doing aggressive things, etc., then our relationships with women will actually improve.

Since 1993, date rape and marital rape have been listed as crimes in all 50 states. The law states that a person needs positive, explicit consent to make contact with another person sexually, or it can be judged rape. Consent must be given voluntarily, freely, and intelligently. Consent cannot be impaired by alcohol or other drugs.

Most states now have special laws setting criminal penalties for domestic physical abuse. One of the most important changes in the law is an exception to the usual requirement that a police officer must witness a misdemeanor in action in order to make an arrest. In all states, an arresting officer responding to a domestic violence call needs only probable cause to believe a crime has been committed. Seeing a woman's injuries will generally suffice for the officer to have probable cause. By statute or policy, most law enforcement officers are required or strongly encouraged to arrest an abuser rather than try to mediate the dispute or require the abuser to leave temporarily.

Until antistalking legislation was passed about 10 years ago, there was little stalking victims could do about their stalkers from a legal standpoint. In some states, the victim had to personally encounter physical harm or damage to property before law enforcement officials could do anything. A restraining order or an order of protection was a victim's only recourse. These required that the stalker stay a certain distance from the victim at home, work, or their children's school or day care center. However, jurisdictional boundaries often limit their enforcement and stalkers can only be penalized after they have violated the order and have seriously hurt or killed their victim.

In 1990, California passed the first antistalking law in the United States. It defined a stalker as someone who "willfully, maliciously, and repeatedly follows or harasses another person and makes a credible threat with the intent to place that person in reasonable fear of death or great bodily injury." This action took place in the wake of the deaths of three California women by stalkers against whom the women had obtained restraining orders. Under the law, a first-time offender who is convicted may be sentenced to up to a year in a county jail, required to pay a fine of up to $1,000, or both.

By 1993, all 50 states and the District of Columbia had passed antistalking legislation. In some states, stalking is treated as a misdemeanor, in others as a felony, and

States' ability to enforce antistalking laws were reinforced when President Bill Clinton signed the Violent Crime Control and Law Enforcement Act of 1994. It includes the Violence Against Women Act, which makes interstate stalking a federal offense.

in others, the first stalking offense is treated as a misdemeanor and subsequent offenses treated as felonies.

Florida is the only state that permits police officers to arrest a suspected stalker without a warrant if there is reason to believe that a crime has occurred. Antistalking laws in Illinois, Hawaii, and Michigan permit the court to require counseling for stalkers, and Michigan offenders can be required to pay for this service themselves. But in a number of cases, the constitutionality of the antistalking law has been questioned. Much of the problem lies in the ambiguity and vagueness of legislation. False accusations are often made by alleged victims, and there is much debate about what constitutes a threat. Furthermore, some argue that the laws may infringe on an individual's right to travel and right to free speech. Still others argue that the laws don't go far enough to protect victims. For example, Illinois law requires there be either two acts of harassment or that the stalker follow the person immediately after making a threat. But by that time, it may be too late for the victim. In Kansas, a person must be both harassed and followed for the stalker to be charged with a crime. And in some states, a victim must believe they will suffer "great bodily harm," while in other states, the stalker must follow through with a threat verbally or in writing for victims to be protected by the law. However, this discounts the fact that many stalkers use symbolic or indirect means to terrorize their victims, such as delivering dead flower bouquets or sending graphic photographs depicting violence.

States' ability to enforce antistalking laws were reinforced when President Bill Clinton signed the Violent Crime Control and Law Enforcement Act of 1994. It includes the Violence Against Women Act, which makes interstate stalking a federal offense. But while antistalking legislation has been helpful in some cases, it is not the only solution in deterring stalkers. The serious psychological problems of some stalkers deserve attention, as well.

ISSUES IN THE FOREFRONT

The Violence Against Women Act was passed by Congress in response to testimony and evidence concerning the burden that gender-motivated violence places on the national economy and the failure of state systems to protect women from violence. Christopher Bailey was the first person to be convicted under the act. He was sentenced to life in prison for kidnapping and beating his wife into a coma.

The Violence Against Women Act of the Violent Crime Control and Law Enforcement Act of 1994 promotes a number of efforts in the criminal justice arena, such as arrests of batterers and those who violate protective orders; coordination of police, prosecutor, and judicial responsibilities for battering cases; and coordination of computer tracking systems for communication among police, prosecutors, and courts. The Violence Against Women Act was passed by Congress in response to testimony and evidence concerning the burden that gender-motivated violence places on the national economy and the failure of state systems to protect women from violence. Members of Congress listened to testimony from women's rights organizations, civil rights organizations, state attorneys general, law professors, law enforcement, physicians, and victims themselves. Provisions of the law are wide ranging. The Violence Against Women Act of 1994 made it a crime to cross a state line to violate a protective order. The law also gives full faith and credit to protective orders, so that an order issued in one state must be enforced in another state.

The act makes rape and domestic abuse a federal crime if the assailants crossed state lines to attack their victims and provides hundreds of millions of dollars for local governments to enforce their own sexual assault laws. A majority of states urged Congress to pass the provision allowing victims to win monetary damages in civil litigation. The act also provides for demonstration grants for coordinating domestic violence programs with the criminal justice system, the social service system, the health care and mental health systems, the education, religious, and business communities, as well as community groups and activities. Grants are also provided for programs to improve training of judges who deal with issues involving domestic violence and to encourage gender bias studies. Also included in the act are increased penalties for federal rape convictions.

The section entitled "Civil Rights for Women" is the most controversial. It establishes a federal civil rights cause of action for victims of violent crimes that were motivated by gender. Under the statute, someone who commits a crime of gender-motivated violence is liable to the injured party and subject to compensatory and punitive damages and injunctive and declaratory relief.

In January 2000, the Supreme Court heard oral arguments in a dispute concerning federal penalties for those who commit crimes against women. The case focuses on a provision of the 1994 Violence Against Women Act that allows women to sue their attackers in federal court for monetary damages. In other words, Congress said the federal government could authorize the lawsuits, which traditionally had been the right of state government. The federal law was based on the federal government's power to regulate interstate

Christy Brzonkala was a Virginia Polytechnic Institute student who claimed she was raped in a dormitory in 1994 by two football players. She sued her attackers in federal court under an interstate commerce provision of the Violence Against Women Act. On May 15, 2000, the Supreme Court ruled 5-4 that victims of sexual assault could not themselves sue assailants in federal court, and that "gender-motivated" crimes are not the kind of economic activity covered by Congress's power to regulate interstate commerce.

commerce and to enforce civil rights and ensure equal protection of the laws. The Supreme Court case was brought by Christy Brzonkala, a Virginia Polytechnic Institute student who claimed she was raped in a dormitory in 1994 by two football players, Antonio J. Morrison and James L. Crawford. In a previous ruling, the U.S. Court of Appeals for the Fourth Circuit had already rejected the congressional reasoning behind the Civil Rights for Women section of the law. Brzonkala's attorneys said that if the Supreme Court agreed with the Fourth Circuit, it would have hampered Congress's power to enforce an individual's constitutional rights and curb its ability to regulate interstate commerce. The Fourth Circuit Court had said Congress's commerce power was limited to regulating activities that are economic in nature.

Brzonkala brought her lawsuit against the two men for the alleged attack after first filing a complaint against them under VPI's sexual assault policy. In the spring of 1995, she pressed charges in the campus judicial system. Neither man was charged with a crime. Crawford contended that he left the room before any sexual activity occurred. He was convicted of an unrelated sexual assault and disorderly conduct. He lost his scholarship and moved home to Florida. A committee found Morrison guilty of sexual assault and suspended him, but after subsequent hearings, his offense was reduced and his punishment was set aside. He received probation and one hour of counseling. He was suspended in 1995 from the football team after being arrested in an unrelated bar brawl and transferred to Hampton University. He later transferred back to Tech and earned a degree in summer 1999. When Brzonkala discovered Morrison was returning to the school, she dropped out and went public with her charges and filed suit. She sued Tech for sex discrimination and the case was settled in February 2000. She was awarded $75,000, but the university admitted no wrongdoing. The Justice Department joined the dispute, *U.S. v. Morrison* on Brzonkala's side.

On May 15, 2000, the Supreme Court ruled 5-4 that victims of sexual assault could not themselves sue assailants in federal court, and that "gender-motivated" crimes are not the kind of economic activity covered by Congress's power to regulate interstate commerce. Brzonkala's attorneys contended that Congress had authority to pass the act based on its constitutional power to regulate interstate commerce. They argued that women who feared being attacked would be hindered from going out at night, taking public transportation or engaging in other activities that would help them find a job and contribute to the economy. Because some of that activity occurs across state lines, Congress believed it had the authority to deter violence against women trying to travel or do business around the country.

The Supreme Court ruling marked the first time since the New Deal era that the court rejected extensive findings by Congress that an activity substantially affects interstate commerce. The power that Congress has under the commerce clause offers lawmakers a means to address problems that federal lawmakers believe states have failed to handle properly on their own. Brzonkala and her attorneys declined to sue the two men in state court under the Violence Against Women Act.

Another critical issue on the legal front involves battered women's syndrome. Much like prisoners of war, or hostages, these women often experience a form of post-traumatic stress disorder that results from the dominance of the male in their relationships and from the batterer's abuse of power. Many battered women live with violence and abuse for years. When they feel their lives or the lives of their children are endangered, they defend themselves by killing or attempting to kill the abusive partner.

Women with BWS cannot distinguish between memories of past abuse and current threats, and thus experience intense feelings of fear and danger. Vivid memories of violence can be triggered spontaneously, and make battered women respond as though the abuse was happening again. Sometimes she remembers what happened to her and sometimes she does not. Her confused thinking and propensity to go off on tangents when telling a story are ways of keeping the memories of the abuse from becoming too painful. This reaction will make the perception of danger from subsequent abuse more vivid. The next time the woman believes violence is imminent, especially if she perceives the danger as life threatening, she may take what she sees as necessary lifesaving actions that she wouldn't take under ordinary circumstances, including killing the batterer. She will likely do this without thinking through the consequences. Her goal is to stop the actual or anticipated attack. Courts may admit testimony about the victim's inability to predict whether what she does will protect her from further abuse—and about the cycle of violence, which includes a tension-building stage, a battering incident, and a period of remorse expressed by the abuser.

Battered women's syndrome was initially introduced at trials as part of a self-defense strategy. Expert witnesses and attorneys usually take a clinical approach to its use. Those who support it being legally recognized argue that battered women's syndrome can be used to educate judges and jurors about violent relationships and the social context in which it existed. One of the objections to battered women's syndrome has been the focus on women's failure to escape rather than on the strategies they use to survive abusive and violent relationships.

Frequently the homicide doesn't meet the legal criteria of self-defense, which includes the following: the honest and reasonable belief that one is in imminent or immediate danger of death or serious bodily harm; that a reasonable amount of force is necessary to avoid danger; and that a reasonable amount of force was used to repel the attack. In a minority of jurisdictions, the defendant must demonstrate the absence of an escape route unless the crime occurred in her or his home. In most jurisdictions, an individual is not legally required to escape from his or her home, but many people expect a woman to leave an abusive relationship and are uneasy when she takes action in self-defense, even if she is in serious danger. Women who claim to have killed their abusers in self-defense must convince juries they reacted in a "reasonable" manner, which is measured in the context of experiences with the abuser and her perceptions at the time of the crime.

In a minority of jurisdictions, "reasonable" is based on legal theory that assumes one person will not ambush another, that combatants will be equally armed, and that both are of equivalent size, strength, and fighting ability. When a woman kills and claims she acted in self-defense, she must show that she honestly and reasonably believed she was in imminent danger of serious bodily harm and that the use of force was necessary to avoid injury or death. If her belief is found to be honest and reasonable and the danger she faced was imminent, then her actions are judged justifiable and she is legally entitled to be acquitted of all charges.

In a second defense strategy, imperfect self-defense, a woman must show she honestly but not reasonably believed she was in imminent danger of serious bodily harm and that the use of force was necessary. This is most likely to be argued in cases of homicides that occurred in nonconfrontational situations. Although the woman's belief that she was in danger may have been authentic, it may be judged by a jury to have been unreasonable. In cases like these, unless jurors are apprised of the history of abuse and the problems a woman experienced in trying to end violence or escape the relationship, they might find the homicide was premeditated.

In the 1981 case of *Smith v. State*, Josephine Smith was charged with murdering her boyfriend. She lived with her boyfriend, the father of her child, on and off for years. One night, Smith returned home late and was confronted by her boyfriend, who made sexual advances toward her. When she told him to stop because she was tired, he shook her and told her not to tell him when to touch her. Later that evening, Smith was kicked in the back by her boyfriend, who also hit her in the head with his fist, grabbed her by the throat, choked her, and threw her against a door. Smith ran and grabbed a gun and tried to call her mother, but her boyfriend had taken the extension phone off the hook. As she fled the apartment, he slammed the door on her foot. Smith fired the weapon three times, eyes closed.

At trial, Smith testified that her partner had beaten her throughout their relationship. She was afraid to leave him because he threatened her. She testified that the beatings increased in frequency when she moved from her mother's home into her own apartment and that after a beating, her partner would apologize. Smith said she didn't call the police or tell her friends because she believed him when he said he would stop beating her. She testified that on the night of the shooting, he had threatened to harm her. She was afraid he was going to hurt her worse than before, so she shot him out of fear for her life. Smith's attorney put a clinical psychologist on the stand whose testimony was ruled inadmissible because the judge believed the jurors could draw their own conclusions as to whether the defendant acted out of fear. The expert explained that it is not uncommon for battered women to fail to report physical abuse to police or their families because they fear intervention by outsiders or being injured. The expert also explained that women who have been battered over many years stay in abusive situations due to low self-esteem and the false belief that the abuse will stop when the abuser promises to stop. The expert tried to explain why Smith didn't leave her abusive situation and described the defendant's psychological reaction to ongoing abuse.

The jury never heard the expert's testimony and Smith was convicted of voluntary manslaughter. She appealed, but the court of appeals upheld the trial court's ruling to exclude the expert's testimony. She appealed again, and the Georgia Supreme Court ruled

the expert testimony was admissible because it didn't interfere with the jury's obligation to determine the facts of the case and was beyond the understanding of the average juror. The judgment was reversed and Smith was acquitted. Following Smith's case, several other states ruled that jurors couldn't be expected to draw conclusions about a defendant's behavior without hearing expert testimony.

Testimony on battered women's syndrome is accepted in courts in every state. Some state legislatures have codified legal decisions about its admissibility and governors have used it to grant clemency to convicted women serving long sentences. Battered women's syndrome is effectively used in criminal court to convict batterers even if the battered woman is unable to testify against them. Family courts make decisions about the validity of property distribution and child custody and visitation arrangements. It has been used to

Testimony on battered women's syndrome is accepted in courts in every state. Some state legislatures have codified legal decisions about its admissibility and governors have used it to grant clemency to convicted women serving long sentences. Battered women's syndrome is effectively used in criminal court to convict batterers even if the battered woman is unable to testify against them.

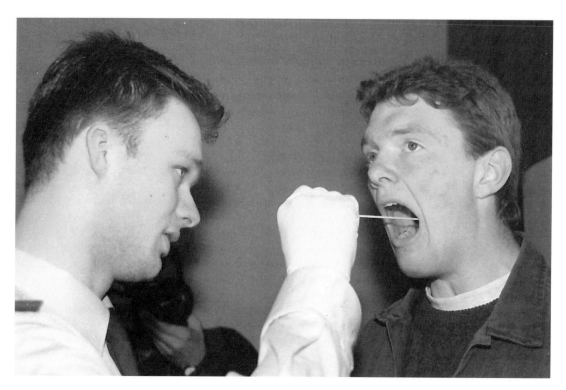

When a suspect is apprehended, a prosecutor can apply for a court order to obtain a DNA sample from an alleged rapist. If the court finds there is probable cause to grant the request for DNA testing, often based on suspect identification through a photo or lineup, a sample is taken from the suspect and submitted to a lab for DNA analysis. If a match is made, DNA analysis can be used to prosecute a case.

deny a batterer rights to property when he has killed a woman after a long history of abuse.

There have been advances in the scientific realm as well as on the legal front. In the 1990s, scientific advances in DNA analysis improved the likelihood of success in prosecuting rape cases. Although the technique is controversial, DNA analysis has proven to be a reliable method of positively identifying and thus convicting sex offenders. DNA analysis is based on the unique nature of each human being's DNA, which is a substance present in blood, saliva, semen, skin, and hair follicles. A DNA molecule contains a person's genetic code, which differs from everyone else's. After a rape, if seminal fluid is left at the crime scene or on the victim's body and is properly collected and preserved, DNA can be extracted from the sample and developed into a "photographic print." Each print shows the different DNA sequences of each chromosome.

When a suspect is apprehended, a prosecutor can apply for a court order to obtain a sample of the alleged rapist's blood for DNA analysis. If the court finds there is probable cause to grant the request for DNA testing, often based on suspect identification through a photo or lineup, the suspect's blood is drawn and submitted to a lab for DNA analysis. If a match is made between the blood sample and seminal fluid, DNA analysis can be used to prosecute a case. DNA evidence is admissible at trials in many courts because it is reliable and accepted in the scientific community.

In Wee Waa, Australia, a 91-year-old woman was brutally raped in 1997 and investigators had no suspects. In attempts to solve the case, police asked all the men in town to submit a DNA sample. About 600 of 612 men complied. In April 2000, a 44-year old farm laborer turned himself in and was charged with the rape. He did comply with the screening, but turned himself in before his sample was analyzed.

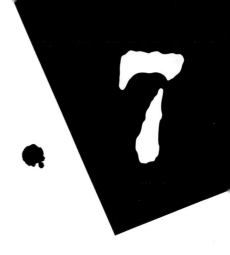

THE SURVIVORS

Victims of domestic violence can suffer long-term effects of abuse such as self-neglect or self-injury; depression, anxiety, panic attacks, and sleep disorders; alcohol and drug abuse; aggression toward themselves and others; chronic pain; eating disorders; sexual dysfunction; and suicide attempts.

Susan's drug-addicted husband, Jim, returned home one night in 1999 in a rage over her recent miscarriage and began punching and kicking her. Susan and her five children were terrified. Susan yelled to one of her sons to call 911 as her husband continued on his rampage. As her son tried to call for help, Jim ripped the phone out of the wall and turned his abuse on the boy. Using a portable phone she was carrying, Susan was able to contact police. Jim was later arrested and is serving time in jail, while Susan and her children try to pick up the pieces. She and her children are in therapy for victims of domestic violence and Susan attends college while holding down a part-time job helping other domestic violence victims.

The damage caused by domestic violence is not limited to the physical bruises or emotional scars of the most recent incident. Victims of domestic violence can suffer long-term effects of abuse such as self-neglect or self-injury; depression, anxiety, panic attacks, and sleep disorders; alcohol and drug abuse; aggression toward themselves and others; chronic pain; eating disorders; sexual dysfunction; and suicide attempts. Shame, guilt, self-hatred, fear, problems with physical intimacy, and anger are common responses of survivors.

After being subjected to physical and emotional abuse, women are systematically stripped of their self-esteem, to the point where they falsely believe they need their batterer to survive, despite the violence. Battered women experience trauma similar to that of rape victims–PTSD–post-traumatic stress disorder characterized by symptoms such as anxiety, depression, nightmares, flashbacks of violent scenarios, and a sense of being detached from their bodies and numb to the physical world. Seldom does the battered woman know when the batterer will strike. She is usually unable to control a violent situation once it starts.

Sometimes years of psychological abuse cause victims to believe they deserve to be treated badly. They may feel defeated by the repeated abuse and feel unable to see a way out, or they may desperately hope that the situation will change. They may fear what the abuser will do if they try to leave. Many women do not leave their abusers because they have no money, have no place to go (or no place that will accept children), and fear losing custody of their children. Sometimes a woman's religious or cultural beliefs may make her husband's abuse seem acceptable.

In 1998, Im Jung Kwuon was a marriage and family counseling intern in Los Angeles. She counseled convicted batterers. Kwuon had suffered from domestic violence and considered her job of helping families to be a part of her recovery process. As a counselor, Kwuon helped run a court-ordered, year-long domestic violence prevention program for men who had beaten or killed their girlfriends or wives. Kwuon explained that as a young adult, she chose boyfriends who were abusive. In one instance, she remembered standing mute when a boyfriend punched a wall. He told her that he was provoked by her anger. She feared that she would be struck next. She learned the hard way that being a paralyzed victim or witness supports abusive behavior. But counseling saved Kwuon's life.

Victims of rape often manifest long-term symptoms of chronic headaches, fatigue, sleep disturbance, recurrent nausea, decreased appetite, eating disorders, menstrual pain, sexual dysfunction, and suicide attempts. In addition, there is evidence to indicate that sexual assault can increase the odds of substance abuse.

Victims of marital or date rape are 11 times more likely to be clinically depressed, and six times more likely to experience social phobia than are nonvictims. Psychological problems are still evident in cases as long as 15 years after the assault.

The adult pregnancy rate associated with rape is estimated to be 4.7 percent, which suggests that there may be 32,101 annual rape-related pregnancies among American women over age 18. Nongenital physical injuries occur in approximately 40 percent of rape cases. Sexually transmitted diseases resulting from rape range from 3.6 percent to 30 percent. About 0.1 percent of all rape cases result in the death of the victim.

Survivors need to know that they are not alone with their pain, that healing is possible, and that whatever the circumstances, the rape was not their fault. Survivors need someone who will care enough to listen without judging them. Survivors of sexual assault have described long-term emotional effects such as grief, anger, fear, lowered self-esteem, helplessness, guilt, shame, sexual dysfunction, body image distortion, and problems in other relationships.

Survivors report strong fear reactions, loss of control, and disrupted lives.

Because the victim of sexual assault frequently knows the attacker, a violation of trust is almost always experienced. Most survivors also report feeling degraded by the experience and stripped of their dignity by the abuser. Often survivors find no social comfort and support after rape or harassment. Those who remain silent feel isolated and begin to view themselves as deviant. Those who reach out to family and friends often offer rejection, blame, or disbelief, rather than support and comfort.

Mary was raped by a man she had dated for just two months. Afterward, she found herself mistrusting friends, coworkers, and people in general. When she told her parents about the devastating incident, they reacted with blame and embarrassment. Mary felt traumatized by her experience and was afraid and ashamed to share with others her terrifying ordeal.

Many emotional responses such as stress behaviors and fear reduce with time and distance from the trauma. However, relationship problems and feelings of guilt, depression, and helplessness may continue or grow worse with time and require more direct intervention. Many survivors have difficulty recognizing their experience as victimization. It is helpful to use the words that fit the experience, validating the depth of the survivor's feelings, and allowing her to feel her experience was serious. In some cases, labeling the experience in the context of being a sexual assault can help a person recognize that they have been the victim of a crime.

Elaine was the victim of extreme domestic violence for 16 years—physically, emotionally, and sexually. Her husband sexually assaulted her in front of the children and in broad daylight in front of the living room window, where the neighbors could see. Elaine sought refuge at an emergency shelter for battered women. She

arrived with no clothes or personal belongings to speak of. Because of the duration and high level of violence perpetrated on Elaine, counselors at the shelter were concerned for both her physical safety and mental health. After all, her husband had threatened to kill her. They provided her with food, clothing and psychiatric and legal counseling.

When Elaine first came to the shelter, she abused alcohol and drugs to ease the pain. She was clinically depressed and chain-smoked packs of cigarettes. Each day, she paced back and forth around the shelter in her coat, clutching her purse. During winter, she sat in her unheated car for hours at a time sneaking

There is evidence to indicate that sexual assault can increase the odds of substance abuse. Survivors of sexual assault have described long-term emotional effects such as grief, anger, fear, lowered self-esteem, helplessness, guilt, shame, sexual dysfunction, body image distortion, and problems in other relationships.

drinks of vodka, but able to conceal her drinking from the counselors.

The years of abuse had severely diminished Elaine physically and mentally. She had survived cancer twice and had a breast removed, which her husband tormented her about afterward. She stayed at the shelter for 18 months; a normal length of stay was 90 days. When Nichelle Mitchem, director of Women Against Abuse, accompanied Elaine to court for the last time (Elaine had expressed an interest in divorc-ing her husband), Elaine proclaimed that the time spent there had been the worst of her life because she had missed her husband. Going to the shelter was analogous to death for Elaine because leaving her husband spelled the end of a relationship she desper-ately believed she needed and wanted. Counselors weren't certain of what happened to Elaine, but more than likely she returned to her abusive husband.

"We were blocking her from his obsession," says Mitchem. "He threatened her. She was brainwashed. This speaks to the diminished sense of self that battered women experience."

It is important for survivors to share their experi-ences with others, whether through group therapy or conversations with trusted friends or associates. Within the group conversation, the victim can discover that others have overcome similar traumas and that her reactions are normal. Survivors must be allowed to grieve over the personal losses caused by the assault, such as the loss of a job or rejection by friends or family after disclosure. The mourning process takes at least a year and involves stages of acute stress, depression, denial, and anger prior to achieving peace with the reality of the loss.

Survivors may continue to suffer from depression and PTSD or substance abuse problems even after they are safe. They may experience feelings of shame after the relationship is over or anger toward their partners.

Some women still feel attached to their partner despite the abuse. Some may have lost their home or custody of their children. Some women may find themselves in a state of financial insecurity. Others are abandoned by friends after their escape. Behavior therapy teaches techniques for coping with losses.

In general, three types of psychological treatment are offered to survivors of violence—crisis intervention counseling, individual follow-up care, and group follow-up care. Crisis intervention counseling is the most widely offered service. Hotlines and telephone counseling are available through government and private agencies or, as in New York City, the police department (Special Victims Unit). Telephone counseling usually involves providing emotional support

It is important for survivors to share their experiences with others, whether through group therapy or conversations with trusted friends or associates. Survivors may seek help from a domestic violence advocacy group or hotline. Survivors must be allowed to grieve over the personal losses caused by the assault.

and practical advice to the survivor and making appropriate referrals. Face-to-face counseling is typically provided by peer rape crisis counselors who provide immediate, nonjudgmental aid and support to the survivor during the acute phase of trauma, when symptoms of PTSD are present.

Crisis intervention counseling takes place in a hospital emergency room or at the site of a community agency to which the survivor has come for care. Rape survivors who don't receive such psychological support are likely to experience traumatic consequences that become more severe and debilitating. Most rape crisis centers offer and recommend short-term follow-up counseling for individuals or groups. Individual counseling is usually provided by a social worker, psychologist, or psychiatrist. Group sessions may be led by a professional or trained peer, who usually establishes a time frame—usually 12 weeks for crisis counseling—or it can be longer. Group therapy doesn't provide the one-on-one attention given to patients in individual counseling, but it does have some advantages. Survivors are likely to feel less isolated and understand more directly that others have had the same experience.

Another form of therapy is provided to the husband, boyfriend, or parents of the rape victim. They can discuss their own feelings about the rape and receive some insight into what the survivor is feeling. Long-term therapy can be beneficial for survivors who experience difficulty in recovery or who have preexisting psychological disorders.

Women Organized Against Rape (WOAR), part of the National Sexual Violence Resource Center, is a Philadelphia-based agency that provides comprehensive services to survivors of sexual abuse and assault and their families. From 1992 to 1993, WOAR responded to 4,677 hotline calls from abuse survivors. An additional 6,047 victim-related calls were received and/or made by WOAR. The agency also provided counseling for 781 victim/survivors and their families in the emergency rooms.

Carole Johnson, executive director of WOAR, says sexual abuse survivors exhibit symptoms commonly associated with post traumatic stress disorder (PTSD), including nightmares, fear of being alone, constant "watchfulness," anxiety, fear of leaving their home, eating disorders, and multiple-personality disorders. Symptoms can also be physical—some survivors mutilate themselves if they've been beaten or mutilated.

"For many women, there are issues with self-worth and self-esteem," said Johnson. "They feel ashamed and dirty. There's self-blame. Rape is about power and control over a person. Rape isn't about sexuality, looking sexual or what a woman is wearing."

Johnson says that fewer than 20 percent of people report being raped because of feelings of embarrassment and shame. Some women come to WOAR even 30 years after their assault because something has triggered their memories or they have experienced flashbacks. These women believe they are able to get over their rape on their own, particularly those who don't want anyone to know.

Ann Gaulin, director of counseling services at WOAR, says treatment of rape involves family support groups and one-on-one and peer-group therapy. Treatment focuses on helping survivors to mentally process the trauma. "We gauge the success of the treatment by how effectively we are able to reduce the long-term effects of PTSD," said Gaulin.

"We teach about domestic violence and provide counseling with victims and perpetrators, as well as prevention," said Nichelle Mitchem of Women Against Abuse. "We've seen kids as young as nine dating and involved in violent behavior."

Both Johnson and Mitchem point to the widespread problem of underreporting of rape and domestic violence and its effect on how violence against women is perceived. In the fall of 1999, the *Philadelphia Inquirer* issued a series of articles on how cases of violence against women have been misclassified as misdemeanors, lesser charges, or even dismissed by the Philadelphia police department. "It gives a distorted picture of the prevalence of crimes against women," said Mitchem. "This is one of the most pressing public issues we have."

According to Mitchem, common effects of domestic abuse include feelings of isolation, diminished self-worth, and delusions that the abuser will change his behavior. Said Mitchem:

> Batterers isolate their victims from friends and family. They tell them they're crazy, unattractive, stupid, worthless and that no one else would want them. In the tension-building phase of the cycle of abuse, the batterer is physically violent—they kick things and throw things so the victim knows harm will come soon. It's a myth that women have control over batterers' behavior, despite his claims in the "honeymoon" phase that "If only you just kept the house clean, or have dinner ready, you'd be fine [and I wouldn't have to hurt you]."

Edith, a client of Women Against Abuse, suffered sexual abuse and battering from her husband over many years. At home, she was filled with terror at the sound of him walking across the wooden floors. Because of this, Edith developed a violent twitch that occurred at least twice every five minutes. The twitching gradually disappeared over the course of a year of counseling, during which time Edith obtained a restraining order and divorced her husband.

When Mitchem worked in legal services in an affluent county in northern New Jersey, she saw divorced women who were abused by their ex-husbands and helped them obtain orders of support in amounts that were ample enough to sustain several families at once, such as $5,000 to $10,000 per month. Yet despite all of their material possessions, these women would allow their abusers back into their lives because of feelings of inadequacy. Said Mitchem:

> These women got the big house, cars, and didn't have to work. But they worried about things like, "How will I pay the bills? How will I make a choice about summer camp? Where will I send the kids for summer vacation?" I thought they only needed emergency housing, legal services to get an order of protection, or financial support. People need emotional support, too. They need empowerment, knowledge and information about the dynamics of domestic violence.

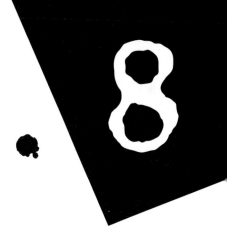

WOMEN AND THE LAW

Today, an abused woman is far more likely to have a complaint handled seriously and to have the abuse considered a crime by legal authorities than 20 years ago. Several police departments, including those in San Francisco and Duluth, Minnesota, have developed programs and written policies to make handling of spousal abuse calls more effective and consistent and to provide guidelines for officers. This includes recognizing that a crime has been committed, arresting the abuser, and providing some form of protection for the victim.

Duluth has been in the forefront with regard to strong antiabuse policies, and aspects of its program have been adopted by other police forces in the United

---

Today, an abused woman is far more likely to have a complaint handled seriously and to have the abuse considered a crime by legal authorities than 20 years ago. Here, a police officer is notified about a domestic violence 911 call.

States. Typically, a first-time offender is sentenced to 30 days in jail and put on probation pending completion of a 26-week batterer's program. Missed classes result in jail time.

By 1992, 15 states, the District of Columbia, and many municipalities had instituted a mandatory arrest policy whenever the police are called in to a domestic violence situation. In Connecticut, where a strict arrest policy is mandatory, the dual arrest rate is 14 percent.

In the 1970s, it was legal for the police to make probable cause, warrantless arrests for felonies, but only 14 states permitted it for misdemeanors. Because simple assault and battery is a misdemeanor in most states, family violence victims were forced to initiate their own criminal charges against the batterer. Today, West Virginia is the only state that doesn't authorize warrantless, probable-cause misdemeanor arrests in domestic violence cases. More than half the states have added qualifiers that require evidence such as visible signs of injury or that the violence be reported within eight hours of the incident. Some police departments have adopted a presumptive arrest policy, whereby an arrest should be made unless there are clear and compelling reasons not to arrest. Proponents say that by arresting abusers, victims have an opportunity to seek help and escape fear.

From 1982 to 1983, Tracey Thurman continually called the police in her hometown of Torington, Connecticut, to report that her estranged husband was repeatedly threatening her and her child's life. The police ignored her requests for help. She tried to file complaints against her husband, but city officials ignored her. The police continued to ignore her pleas for help even after Tracey's husband was arrested for attacking her in view of a policeman. A judge issued a protection order forbidding him to go to his wife's home, but her husband violated the order and came to

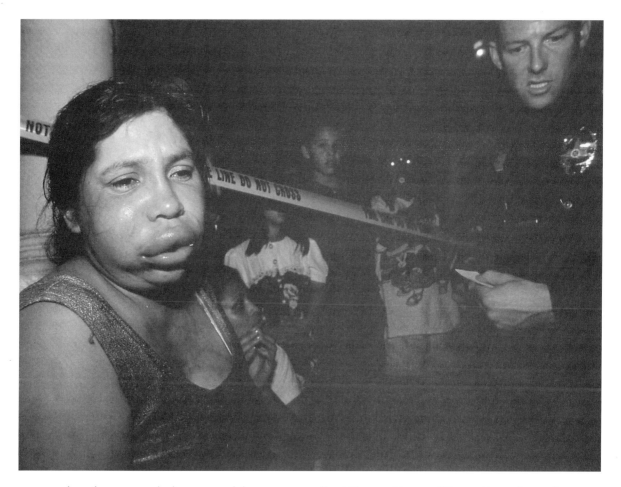

her house and threatened her repeatedly. The police ignored her when she asked them to arrest her husband for violating his probation and for threatening her life. She obtained a restraining order against her husband, which he violated, but the police continued to ignore her.

On one fateful day, June 10, 1983, Thurman's husband came to her house, and she called the police. He stabbed her over and over in the chest, neck, and throat. Approximately 25 minutes later, a police officer arrived but didn't arrest him despite his attacks. Three more police officers showed up as Thurman's husband grabbed their son and threw him down on Thurman,

When police arrive on the scene of a domestic dispute they must be prepared for anything. Many municipalities have instituted a mandatory arrest policy whenever the police are called in to such a situation. Proponents say that by arresting abusers, victims have an opportunity to seek help and escape fear.

who was bleeding profusely. He was still not arrested and was walking around freely. While Thurman lay prone on a stretcher awaiting an ambulance, her husband came at her again and kicked her in the head, causing permanent injury. The police finally arrested her husband and took him into custody. Thurman sued the City of Torington, claiming she was denied equal protection under the law. A federal court jury awarded Thurman $2.3 million in compensatory damages. The state of Connecticut changed its law, calling for the arrest of abusive spouses. In the year following the new law, the number of arrests for domestic assault almost doubled from 12,400 to 23,830.

Still, spouse abuse cases are often plagued with problems of evidence because domestic violence is conducted in secret. Society's changing attitudes toward abuse also influence the response of those in the judicial system. In many cases of abuse, many still feel that abuse is preferable to breaking up the family.

Some claim that if courts helped women file charges and supported them, many more would follow through. In Quincy, Massachusetts, the court system has a separate office for restraining orders and support groups for women. As a result, only 2.8 percent of women fail to appear at their court hearing.

In 1974, the Justice Department created the Law Enforcement Assistance Administration, which provided funding to states and cities for projects in the criminal justice field. As a result, the Sex Crimes Prosecution Unit of the New York County District Attorney's Office was created in 1974 to treat the special needs and unique problems of sex-crime victims. It was the first of its kind in the United States.

The unit has grown exponentially since then and has become a permanent part of the district attorney's office. This innovative unit implemented a Sex Crimes Analysis Unit, to facilitate and encourage reporting of sexual abuse cases, and a detective unit in each of New York's five boroughs to specialize in the investigation of sexual assault cases. A key feature of the unit is the recognition that survivors of sexual assault require treatment different from that required by other crime victims. In addition, because prosecuting sex offenses is more difficult than other felony crimes, victims need to be made more comfortable throughout the process and they need to understand and to present arguments that more directly address jurors' concerns, which include why rape occurs. A majority of states, the District of Columbia, and Puerto Rico have passed laws that permit people in many different relationships to the abuser, such as relatives of the victim, couples in dating relationships, and ex-spouses, to file for protection orders. Petitioners can file for protection orders in cases of physical abuse, sexual assault, marital rape, harassment, emotional abuse and stalking.

For victims of stalking, protection orders are the only legal recourse to control the perpetrator's threatening behavior. In the 1990s, all 50 states and the District of Columbia enacted some form of anti-stalking law. Research shows that about 200,000 victims have been threatened by stalking. The Fulton County Victim Assistance Program in Atlanta and Citizens Against Stalking in Richmond, Virginia, provide services to about 600 victims of domestic violence each month.

There are many local domestic violence agencies that can provide crisis services such as shelter, counseling, and legal assistance. On February 21, 1996, President Clinton announced the National Domestic Violence Hotline, 1-800-799-SAFE, a nationwide, 24-hour, toll-free domestic violence hotline. It provides immediate crisis intervention resources, including counseling and referrals to community resources such as emergency services and shelters. It also provides assistance in reporting abuse to survivors of

There are many domestic violence agencies that can provide crisis services such as shelter, counseling, and legal assistance. Hotlines like 1-800-33-HAVEN and 1-800-799-SAFE, can provide immediate crisis intervention resources, including counseling and referrals to community resources such as emergency services and shelters.

domestic violence, family members, neighbors, and the general public.

One of the most important developments to help abused women is the creation of shelters to offer them refuge. Safe houses and refuges have become the symbol of help for battered women. In 1971, Erin Pizzey founded the first known refuge for battered women, the Chiswick Women's Aid in London. Since then, shelters have spread throughout the United States, Canada, and Europe.

Shelters help women regain power over their lives and offer economic and social support, as well as care and understanding. The abused woman who seeks refuge at a shelter can identify with other women like herself who believe her story, offer understanding, are committed to her safety, and value her. From these relationships, battered women gain confidence to live violence-free lives and form a

more accurate assessment of themselves and their batterer. At the shelter, a battered woman is no longer isolated, which previously had led to her inaction and acceptance of her plight. Shelters play a critical role in helping members of medical staffs, social services, and law enforcement in the community better serve victims, children, and abusers.

Shelters can provide local referrals to legal aid, shelters, and other services. Many local agencies like Philadelphia's Women Against Abuse provide shelter for women in crisis situations—women being stalked,

Safe houses and refuges have become the symbol of help for battered women. In 1971, Erin Pizzey founded the first known refuge for battered women, the Chiswick Women's Aid in London. Since then, shelters have spread throughout the United States, Canada, and Europe.

beaten or threatened, or assistance through community programs. At the shelter, women can get food, clothing, support and counseling, legal aid, and assistance in finding a job. Community programs offer support groups, individual counseling, legal aid, education, literature on other regional agencies, abuse-prevention programs for teens, suggestions of therapists who deal with battered women, a treatment program for drug and alcohol abuse, parenting programs where children can receive counseling with mothers, and access to family-law clinics where women can receive free legal consultation. Today, every state has a Coalition Against Domestic Violence that provides referrals to the nearest shelter and lobbies for better laws and services for battered women.

The U.S. Centers for Disease Control has awarded $1.5 million each to four cities (Milwaukee, Houston, Duluth, and Atlanta) for use in finding ways to curb violence against women. In Milwaukee a project called Safe at Home provides a media blitz of abuse-prevention advertisements and presentations to thousands of children and adults. The project has generated an increase in phone calls to abuse hotlines and the formation of community citizen groups banded together to stop the violence. Houston's Department of Health and Human Services was awarded funds for a mentoring project for abused pregnant women to reduce the amount of postpartum abuse at local health clinics. In Duluth, the Duluth Domestic Violence Prevention Project, an interagency network, used funds to enhance and expand intervention services for domestic abuse victims and batterers. Goals include improving the coordination and communication on cases and computerizing the tracking of cases. The Domestic Abuse Intervention Project is a coordinated community response that includes 911, the jail, police, probation officers, prosecutors, mental health agencies, and victim services. It has expanded to include additional parts of the criminal justice system, public health, employee assistance providers and county child protection workers. In Atlanta, Men Stopping Violence received funds to implement and evaluate a community intervention project to reduce domestic violence against women by focusing on changing the criminal justice response to the abuse of women. This includes a batterers' program as an alternative to jail, training of law enforcement officers about battering, and a media campaign to raise community awareness about domestic violence. Goals include educating the public about arrest policies, self-protective options, such as restraining orders, separation, and seeking safe haven in battered women's shelters.

In the private sector, a group of companies in Massachusetts are tackling a problem businesses have been reluctant to confront, domestic violence. Employers Against Domestic Violence began in 1997 as a series of lunchtime discussions among several Boston companies about how to protect employees from abusive husbands and boyfriends. Today, the group is a formal nonprofit organization with 28 private corporations among its members, along with government, police, and advocacy groups.

Employers Against Domestic Violence has helped launch similar programs in New York City and Indianapolis. The group has helped women like Cary, who was trying to keep her two children away from her abusive husband, who threatened to kill the whole family. Cary's employer sent security officers to accompany her to court and to guard her house. Her employer also promised to help her leave the state if necessary, and provided therapy on company time.

Although few rape-prevention initiatives have been evaluated, there are programs with strategies that have promise for rape prevention, such as The Safe Dates Program. The Safe Dates Program is a school-based curriculum that targets gender-role stereotyping, dating violence norms, conflict management skills, help-seeking, and cognitive factors associated with help-seeking. The Safe Dates curriculum is designed specifically for middle school-aged youth to help them develop positive attitudes and skills to ensure healthy relationships and to prevent interpersonal violence. The program's goals include reducing the number of teens who report incidences of dating violence and increasing family, school, and community support for education regarding the prevention of dating violence. In-class activities include a theater production performed by peers, a 10-session curriculum, and a poster contest. Community activities include special services for teens in violent relationships and community service-provider training.

Perhaps the best preventative measure of rape is its eradication. If more cases of sexual abuse and assault were reported to the police, perhaps society would recognize that this is a type of violence that is disproportionately directed toward women, and take measures to end this crime. As it stands, many rapists don't think there are consequences for their behavior. Typically, the criminal justice system does not believe the word of a rape survivor. Given the fact that we are not able to deal honestly and directly with this issue, changing attitudes and behavior is difficult. But it is incumbent on the part of victims to break the cycle of sexual abuse, to go public and report these crimes, so that others—social workers, courts, schools, police— can get involved in reducing the incidence of this crime. It can start by contacting a crisis center or calling a hotline to seek advice on what to do. Perpetrators also have a role in breaking the cycle. They must examine their behavior and attitudes about women and consider the consequences of their actions. Men who view or treat women as sexual objects allow rape to happen. Changing laws won't stop rape—changing people's lifestyles, attitudes, and behavior will.

Although husbands can no longer legally beat their wives and wives can legally sue their husbands for damages, wife beating hasn't disappeared. It has remained a reality for many women who, despite the recent legal changes, still feel trapped with nowhere to go for help and with little chance of support from existing legal institutions. Once hidden behind curtains, the problem of wife abuse has come into the open as women have become increasingly conscious of their rights. With expanded awareness and support, the increased alternatives for battered women offer them greater opportunities.

Bibliography

American Medical Association. Http://www.ama-assn.org.

Baker, Kimberly B. "DA says kidnapped woman 'still alive'." *Boston Globe*, February 8, 1992.

Biskupic, Joan. "States role at issue in rape suit." *Washington Post*, January 10, 2000.

————. "Justices reject lawsuits for rape." *Washington Post*, May 16, 2000.

Brownmiller, Susan. *Against Our Will: Men, Women and Rape.* New York: Fawcett Columbine, 1975.

Bode, Janet. *Voices of Rape.* Danbury, Conn.: Frankin Watts, 1998.

Boumil, Marcia Mobilia, J.D., L.L.M., Friedman Joel, Ph.D., Taylor, Barbara Ewert, J.D.

Date Rape: The Secret Epidemic-What it is, what it isn't, what it does to you, what you can do about it. Deerfield Beach, Fla.: Health Communications, Inc., 1993.

Burgess, Ann Wolbert, editor. *Rape and Sexual Assault.* New York: Garland Publishing, 1985.

Centers for Disease Control and Prevention. Http://www.cdc.gov.

Chambers, Veronica. "Rape and a road back: a survivor's brave story." *Newsweek*, October 12, 1998.

Delgado, Luz. "Woman is shot dead in driveway. Daughter said to be abducted." *Boston Globe*, February 7, 1992.

————. "Search continues for Waltham man." *Boston Globe*, February 11, 1992.

————. "Kidnap victim free; suspect in standoff." *Boston Globe*, February 12, 1992.

————. "An explosive contradiction comes to an end in Brockton." *Boston Globe*, February 13, 1992.

Domestic Violence: The Facts, a manual published by the Massachusetts Committee on Criminal Justice and Peace at Home, Inc.

Bibliography

Dworkin, Andrea. *Life and Death: Unapologetic Writing on the Continuing War against Women.* New York: The Free Press, 1997.

Family Violence Prevention Fund. Http://www.fvpf.org

Fairstein, Linda. *Sexual Violence: Our War Against Rape.* New York: William Morrow & Co., 1993

Felder, Raoul and Barbara Victor. *Getting Away with Murder.* New York: Simon & Schuster, 1996.

Gagné, Patricia. *Battered Women's Justice: The Movement for Clemency and the Politics of Self-Defense.* New York: Twayne Publishers, 1998.

Gerdes, Louise. *Battered Women.* San Diego: Greenhaven Press, 1999.

Goetting, Ann. *Getting Out: Life Stories of Women Who Left Abusive Men.* New York: Columbia University Press, 1999.

Goodman, Ann. "Answering their call: Verizon Wireless' Denny Strigl and the victims of domestic abuse." *Sky,* July 2000.

Henson, Rich. "Domestic abuse death toll soars in rural Berks County." *The Philadelphia Inquirer,* April 23, 2000.

Jacobson, Neil, Ph.D. and John Gottman, Ph.D. *When Men Batter Women: New Insights into Ending Abusive Relationships.* New York: Simon & Schuster, 1998.

Kahn, Joseph P. "Strong, not silent." *Boston Globe,* April 27, 2000.

Kaye, Judith S. "Making the case for hands-on courts." *Newsweek,* October 1, 1999.

Kwon, Im Jung. "Facing down abusers," *Newsweek,* August 10, 1998.

Landau, Elaine. *Stalking.* Danbury, Conn.: Franklin Watts, 1996.

Landes, Alison B., Mark Siegel, MA, Ph D., Carol D. Foster. *Domestic Violence: No Longer Behind the Curtains.* Wylie, Tex.: Information Press, 1993.

Landes, Alison B., Suzanne Squyres, editors. *Violent Relationships: Battering and Abuse Among Adults.* Wylie, Tex.: Information Press, 1997.

Bibliography

Ledray, Linda E., R.N., Ph.D. *Recovering From Rape*. New York: Henry Holt and Company, 1994.

Madriz, Esther. *Nothing Bad Happens to Good Girls: Fear of Crime in Women's Lives*. Berkeley and Los Angeles, Calif.: University of California Press, 1997.

"Many firms fight domestic abuse," *The Associated Press*, April 16, 2000.

Masters, Brooke A. "'No winners' in rape lawsuit." *Washington Post*, May 20, 2000.

McGrory, Brian. "Murder-kidnap suspect kills self: Gunshot ends ordeal as police storm house." *Boston Globe*, February 13, 1992.

McCuen, Gary E. *Pornography and Sexual Violence*. Hudson, Wis.: Gary E. McCuen Publications, Inc., 1985.

National Violence Against Women Prevention Research Center, Http://www.violenceagainstwomen.org.

No Safe Place: Violence Against Women, a PBS documentary film. Written and co-produced by Mary Dickson. Produced and directed by Colleen Casto. Airdate March 27, 1998.

O'Toole, Laura L. and Jessica R. Schiffman, editors. *Gender Violence: Interdisciplinary Perspectives*. New York: New York University Press, 1997.

Robinson, Lauren. "Courts urged to check past of batterers." *Boston Globe*, February 14, 1992.

Sigesmund, B.J. "Rape ads target men." *Newsweek*, October 28, 1998.

Sunday, Suzanne R. and Ethel Tobach. *Violence against Women*. New York: Gordian Press, 1985.

U.S. Department of Justice. Http://www.ojp.usdoj.

U.S. Department of Justice, Office of Justice Programs, 1995. (Bureau of Justice Statistics Special Report, no. NCJ-154348). *National Crime Victimization Survey for 1992-1993*.

U.S. Department of Justice, Office of Justice Programs, 2000. (Bureau of Justice Statistics Special Report, no. NCJ-182734). *Criminal Victimization 1999: Changes 1998-99 with Trends 1993-99.*

Umhoefer, Dave. "Dating violence doesn't disturb many teens." *Milwaukee Journal Sentinel*, April 26, 2000.

Warren, Steven. "Be open to the idea of DNA as crime fighting tool." *The Arizona Republic*, April 27, 2000.

Wekesser, Carol, editor. *Pornography.* San Diego; Greenhaven Press, 1997.

Wilson, K.J., Ed.D. *When Violence Begins at Home: A Comprehensive Guide to Understanding and Ending Domestic Abuse.* Alameda, Calif.: Hunter House Inc., 1997.

Winkler, Kathleen. *Date Rape: A Hot Issue.* Berkeley Heights, N.J.: Enslow Publishers, Inc., 1999.

Women's Rural Advocacy Programs, Http://www.letswrap.com.

Index

Index

and murder, 24
and myths, 30, 41-42,
   49-50, 52-55, 63, 64
and pornography, 41,
   42-44
prevention of, 117-119
and reports to police,
   30, 105-106, 118
and stranger rape, 24, 54
survivors of, 99-100,
   103-106
and Violence Against
   Women Act, 83, 85-89
and women as provokers
   of, 52-53
See also Date rape; Rapists
Rapists, 62-66
and arrest, 79-80
and power and control
   issues, 64, 65-66,
   79, 105
profile of, 53, 54-55,
   63, 79
and rape as revenge,
   64-65
and rape myths, 63, 64

and rape prevention,
   118-119
and testosterone, 64
treatment for, 78-83
warning signs of, 65
See also Date rape; Rape;
   Stalking
Restraining orders, 21-22,
   57, 78, 86, 106, 111,
   112, 113
Roby, C. Y., 54, 64, 65
Rohypnol, 28-29

Safe At Home, 27-28
Safe Dates Program,
   117-118
Sanchez, Ron, 79
Santiago, Carlos Angel
   Diaz, 21
Schaeffer, Rebecca, 22-23
Selective Serotonin Reup-
   take Inhibitors, 75
Self v. Self, 39
Serotonin, 75
Sex Crimes Prosecution Unit
   (New York), 112-113

Shelters, 18, 40, 47, 51,
   100-102, 114-116
Simpson, Nicole Brown,
   13-15, 61
Simpson, O. J., 13-15, 61
Smith, Josephine, 91-93
Smith v. State, 91-93
Stalking, 14, 24, 61
celebrity, 22-23
laws against, 81-83, 113
Steinberg, Joel, 31-33

Telephone counseling,
   103-104
Thurman, Tracey, 110-112

U.S. v. Morrison, 88-89

Victimization rates, fear of
   crime *versus*, 15-16
Violence Against Women
   Act, 83, 85-89

Wertz, Candace, 21, 22, 23

Picture Credits

GERDA GALLOP-GOODMAN is the managing editor of a Philadelphia-based health magazine and a freelance writer living in Philadelphia.

AUSTIN SARAT is William Nelson Cromwell Professor of Jurisprudence and Political Science at Amherst College, where he also chairs the Department of Law, Jurisprudence and Social Thought. Professor Sarat is the author or editor of 23 books and numerous scholarly articles. Among his books are *Law's Violence*, *Sitting in Judgment: Sentencing the White Collar Criminal*, and *Justice and Injustice in Law and Legal Theory*. He has received many academic awards and held several prestigious fellowships. He is President of the Law & Society Association and Chair of the Working Group on Law, Culture and the Humanities. In addition, he is a nationally recognized teacher and educator whose teaching has been featured in the *New York Times*, on the *Today* show, and on National Public Radio's *Fresh Air*.